Discover
HEALING
and
Freedom

Discover
HEALING
and
Freedom

BY
PETER HORROBIN
FOUNDER AND
INTERNATIONAL DIRECTOR
ELLEL MINISTRIES

Sovereign World

Sovereign World Ltd
Ellel Grange
Bay Horse
Lancaster
Lancashire LA2 0HN
United Kingdom

www.sovereignworld.com
Twitter: @sovereignworld
Facebook: www.facebook.com/sovereignworld

ISBN: 978-1-85240-847-3
Kindle 978-1-85240-848-0

Cover design by Zaccmedia.com
Typeset by Graeme Andrew Envydesign Ltd.
Printed and bound in Great Britain by Bell and Bain Ltd, Glasgow

Contents

Preface

1. *Getting Started*   14

*Discovering your first steps to wholeness,
starting from where you are now!*

The journey of life	14
Ways in which I can be "sick"	17
Being honest with God	21
God loves me as I am – learning to trust	22
Him for my future	

2. Who is God and Who am I?   27

Discovering God's foundations for the journey of your life!

Who is God? Understanding the foundations   29
    of our faith
Who am I? Understanding ME!   32
Why do I need Jesus to help me?   33
Making Jesus Lord   35

3. Rebuilding Life – God's Way   39

Discovering the God who loves and heals

His way – or my way?   39
Giving everything to God – the good, the bad   43
    and the ugly!
Discovering God's order for mankind   45
Choosing to live my life God's way   48

4. Forgive and be Forgiven   53

Discovering the joy of forgiveness

Getting my slate clean   55
Forgiving me   58
Forgiving others   59
'Forgiving' God   61

5. *Rejected No More!*   65

Discovering God's unconditional love

Accepting God – as He is!   67

Just as I am – I come!   68

Knowing, accepting and loving myself   69

Accepting others   71

6. Setting the Captives Free!   75

Discovering freedom from Satan's control!

Introducing deliverance   75

How Satan can influence and control our lives   78

Jesus came to set the captives free   80

Healing through deliverance   82

7. Healing for My Relational Past   87

Discovering healing from wrong relationships

Understanding God's created order for relationships   89

The consequences of sexual sin   91

Being honest with myself   99

Restored in the image of God   97

8. _Broken through Wounding and Pain_   99
Discovering healing from the traumas
of the past

How trauma locks us into past experiences   101
Jesus came to heal the broken-hearted   103
Letting God in to my broken past   105
Healing from the consequences of accidents   106

9. _Freedom from Fear_   111
Discovering freedom from the fears
that control

Good and bad fears!   113
The roots and causes of harmful fears   115
Learning to live in a new way   112
Fear free!   118

10. _Learning to Live Again_   123
Discovering God's purposes for your life

Forgetting what's behind   125
Discovering God's purpose for my life   127
Pressing on towards the goal   128
Realising my destiny   129

Epilogue and Afterword   133

Preface

Right at the outset of our journey of discovery, I want to encourage you to look forward to all that God has in store for you. This is a journey that will bring great blessing into your life. For thirty-five years Ellel Ministries has been showing people how to experience God's hope, God's healing and God's restoration. We have seen first-hand, on hundreds of occasions, how Jesus can heal the broken-hearted, set the captives free and equip them for all that lies ahead in their lives.

Long before Jesus came, Isaiah prophesied that the Sovereign Lord would bring God's healing to His people. In these amazing words Isaiah described exactly what Jesus would do:

> *"The Spirit of the Sovereign Lord is on me, because the*
> *Lord has anointed me* **to preach good news to the poor.** *He*
> *has sent me* **to bind up the broken-hearted, to proclaim**
> **freedom for the captives and release from darkness for the**
> **prisoners,** *to proclaim the year of the Lord's favour and the*

> *day of vengeance of our God, to comfort all who mourn and*
> *provide for those who grieve in Zion – to bestow on them a*
> *crown of beauty instead of ashes, the oil of gladness instead*
> *of mourning, and a garment of praise instead of a spirit of*
> *despair. They will be called oaks of righteousness, a planting*
> *of the Lord for the display of his splendour."* (Isaiah 61:1-3)

These wonderful promises still hold good today and are vitally relevant for every single believer who wants to follow Jesus.

God's message of salvation was incredibly good news! It was *free* (good news for the poor!). It was **healing** for the broken-hearted. It was **God's favour** for the hurting and the distressed. It was **freedom** for those who were living their lives in spiritual darkness and bondage. It was **comfort and gladness** for those who mourn. And it brought the **beauty of God's restoration** to those who have been devastated by the events of life or are in despair. **This is the heart of the Gospel. This is the healing and freedom that Jesus offers. We are all in need of His healing!**

And the amazing promise at the end of this Scripture, is that even those who have been long-devastated can become *"oaks of righteousness"* – a living demonstration of the healing love of God, displaying the splendour of the Almighty in the restored lives of His children.

One of God's precious promises says that He will restore to us the years that the locust has eaten (Joel 2:25) – which means that even where there has been devastation there is hope of restoration. God cannot change the facts of our history, but He specialises in healing the consequences of the past and giving back to us in abundance – often over and above anything and everything we have lost and far beyond our expectation (Ephesians 3:20).

It has been such a privilege to see Him do just that for people all over the world. People from all ethnic groups, from all sorts of backgrounds and on countless occasions. I am not talking about God only loving, healing and restoring a privileged few, but declaring that all who come to Him are privileged to be able to enjoy everything He has prepared for them. This is for YOU!

All that He requires of us is a humble and willing heart and a desire to understand and apply in our lives what Jesus taught us. The first disciples were, simply, followers of Jesus who, in turn, became disciple-makers. And ever since that time, Jesus has been inviting those who love and trust Him to follow Him and walk in His footsteps, just as the first disciples did. So, where do I begin?

Start from Where You are!

When you look at a map to plan a journey you need two reference points. The place you're going to and the place where you now are. Both are essential. Unless you know where you are on the map, you will not be able to plan a route to your destination. And the map will be useless! It's only because the SatNav (GPS) on your car knows exactly where you are, that it can show you the way to your destination.

In just the same way, you may look ahead and decide what you want to do with the rest of your life, but unless you know where you are right now, you won't know how to get there. We need God to show us. Where you are on your personal journey through life has been influenced, one way or another, by what has already happened on the road you have travelled so far.

Each one of us carries memories of both blessings and pain – the good and the bad. Unhealed wounds from the past can be today's stumbling blocks, which have the effect of limiting our future. And if our family history, and life's experiences, have left us in need of healing, then without that healing need being met, our vision for the future could be clouded, our fruitfulness restricted and life's realities could fall well short of our dreams and expectations.

While Christian healing does embrace prayer for the healing of physical conditions, it is much wider in its application and significance. And just as a medical doctor needs to know what's wrong with us, physically, before he can start treating a physical condition, we need to know if there is anything spiritually out of order, so that we can find out how it can be put right. We can then start our journey towards the wholeness and freedom that God promises in His Word.

The objective of *Discover Healing and Freedom* is to help you apply God's life-changing keys to your own life and situation – keys that will unlock many of the problems that people face in the ordinary events of daily life. They are keys which will help you establish a solid foundation for all the years that lie ahead of you.

I pray that wherever you are and whatever your personal circumstances may be, that you will find *Discover Healing and Freedom* to be a rich and life-transforming blessing.

Peter Horrobin
Ellel Grange,
Spring 2021

CHAPTER 1

Getting Started

Discovering your first steps to wholeness – starting from where you are now!

The Journey of Life

Life is a journey. None of us can remember the actual moment when life began for us and none of us knows when our life on Earth will come to an end. Right now, we're all somewhere in between these two extremes. Some are nearer the beginning and others are closer to the end.

There is a life that we have already lived and there's a life yet to be lived – a life that, with God's help, we can really look forward to with eager anticipation, irrespective of how young or old we are or what our experiences of life have been so far!

Our experiences to date – good ones, bad ones and the in-between ones – have all contributed to our present situation. Family background, work experience, relationships, traumas, jobs, achievements, difficulties and blessings, opportunities, medical or psychological problems, sicknesses, tragedies, friends, enemies, and a hundred and one other factors, have all played a part in our personal journey through life.

But, so have our reactions to all these things as well – how we have responded to the things that have happened to us can sometimes be as influential and significant as the things themselves! We are changed by our experiences and also by our reactions to them – and, sadly, we are not always changed for the better.

The most profound definition of Christian healing we know is simply **the restoration of God's order in a person's life.** So, throughout *Discover Healing and Freedom*, we are asking God to show those places in our lives which have become disordered – through our parenting (things we have inherited), what we have experienced from others or what we have chosen to do ourselves. We need to bring them all to Jesus, the Healer, and ask Him to restore His order into each area of our life, one step at a time. And when you've taken even just a few steps, you will be surprised at just how far you've travelled!

The Beginning of Life

Though we generally celebrate our first day of independent life as our birthday, life actually began for us at conception. At that moment, we were an embryonic human being, with a spirit, a soul and a body. And we were either male or female. God gave our bodies the gift of life, together with the masterplan (the DNA) for everything that would be necessary for our physical growth and development – all the way through to adulthood.

In Genesis 1:26-27 we are told that God created man in His own image and likeness. It's as if God looked in a mirror and designed the most special part of His creation to look like Him. All the animals and every other living creature were made as unique new creations in their own image and likeness (Gen.1:25) – but God made human beings to be a reflection of Himself!

Genesis 2:7 tells us that God made physical man out of the 'earth' that He had created (our human body). He breathed life into the body (the human spirit) and that man became a living being (human soul). Just as there are three unique dimensions to God – Father, Son and Holy Spirit, there are three unique dimensions to man – spirit, soul and body.

Although we have a human spirit, a soul and a body, we don't conclude that we are three different people. Each of us is a single human being. This mirrors the nature of the Godhead. Because there are three dimensions to God also – Father, Son and Holy Spirit – we don't conclude that there are three Gods. We are three in one, just as God is!

So, you are a unique human being, living at one and the same time in three different ways as your own person (soul), empowered by a human spirit and living within the confines of a physical body. God intended that your spirit, your soul and your body should always be in harmony with each other, just as God the Father, Jesus the Son and Holy Spirit are always in harmony with each other. Jesus said, for example, *"I and my Father are one."* (John 10:30).

What Went Wrong?

Things were radically changed, however, by what happened at the Fall – the moment when man chose to go his own way, independent of God. God had created man to have authority over planet Earth (Genesis 1:27-28).

But when man submitted to Satan's temptation to doubt what God had said, he chose to obey Satan rather than obey God. And when you obey someone else you are putting all your own authority under their control. So, after the Fall, instead of man being in authority over the Earth and everything in it, Satan now took charge and used man, with his God-given authority, to fulfil his own rebellious purposes.

Satan, therefore, took over and he became known as the god of this world (2 Corinthians 4:4). The whole world has, ever since, been under the control of the Evil One (1 John 5:19) and in rebellion against the living God. As a result, mankind has become heir to all the consequences of sin and has been paying the price for the Fall ever since!

Man's Need of Healing

When Paul was writing to the Thessalonians, he prayed that they may be made whole in spirit, in soul and in body (1 Thess. 5:23). Clearly, if Paul was praying for wholeness in each of these areas, he was saying that there could be unwholeness (or sickness) in the spirit, the soul and the body. From this we realise that when praying for someone, it is helpful to know in which area of their being they are sick, so that our prayers can be targeted at the source of the problem and not just at the symptoms.

When David wrote in Psalm 103:1, *"Praise the Lord, O my soul, all my inmost being, praise his holy name"*, it's clear that one part of David was addressing another. David's spirit was addressing his soul and telling it to praise God. And then, in verse 3, David declares to his soul that it is God who forgives all your sins and heals all the diseases that can affect the soul and then the body. The sin choice may be in the soul, but the consequence can also be experienced as physical symptoms in the body.

And in Psalm 51, in which David is confessing to God his sexual sin of adultery with Bathsheba, he describes some of the symptoms that he is experiencing and the places in which he needs healing. In verse 10 he asks God to heal his spirit – *"renew a steadfast spirit within me"* (v.10) and restore his spiritual relationship with God (verses 11 and 12), which means his spirit was sick. He asks God to heal his soul – to cleanse him and create in him a pure heart (verses 7 and 10). And in verse 8 he is crying out for physical healing – *"let the bones you have crushed rejoice"*. As a result of his sin, David was experiencing sickness in his spirit, soul and body and needed healing in every place to which the 'sickness' had spread.

So, in both the New and the Old Testaments we have evidence of sickness being possible in each area of our being.

Ways in which I can be "sick"

In just the same way as Doctors need to know which part of our body is sick, so that they can be specific in the physical treatment they give, we need to know where there is disorder in our lives, so that we can address the problem specifically and deal with the real issue.

Sickness of the Human Spirit

The human spirit is the creative life force which God gave to us at our conception. It's the very core of who we are and through which we relate and have fellowship with Him. When we sin, our relationship with God is damaged and we become sick in our spirit, which then seriously affects our ability to relate with and hear from God. Equally, when we are sinned against by others, the spiritual pain can be very deep. Satan uses our own sins to further interfere with our relationship with God; and the sins of others to penetrate our spiritual defences and cause us inner pain.

Because of the original sin of mankind, which gave Satan spiritual authority in the world, man became separated from God, death became his inheritance and Satan gained the right to interfere in our lives.

When Jesus was talking to Nicodemus (John 3) He explained how He had come into the world to overcome the darkness of sin, so that sinners may be saved. He explained that we each need to be born again so that, as redeemed sinners, we can have a renewed spiritual life, back in fellowship with the God who had made us. Being born again is the primary healing that every one of us needs and without which we cannot know God – we can only know about Him. Being born again is, literally, a resurrection from the dead bringing restoration of our relationship with God. It is the gateway to both our eternal salvation and to all healing that comes from God.

Even when we are born again, our spirit can still be hurt, crushed or broken through things that have happened to us in life, often when we were young. And even as believers we can be tempted and are prone to sin. When that happens we feel dirty (the same sort of guilt and shame that Adam and Eve felt in the Garden which made them want to cover themselves up – Genesis 3:7). It is as if there is a dark cloud overhead and our view of God becomes restricted until the relationship is restored through repentance and forgiveness (1 John 1:9).

Sickness of the Soul

There are three primary dimensions to our soul life – *our mind*, with which we think, *our emotions* with which we sense, feel and respond to what is going on around us, and then ***our will***, with which we make decisions. We can be sick in any or all of these different aspects of our inner being.

Sometimes the things that we have suffered have become too much for us and our ability to cope with the circumstances has been overwhelmed. It can feel as though something has snapped inside. We can try and cope as best we can, but it is often years later that we get to the point of not being able to cope anymore with the unresolved inner pain and start looking for medical, psychological or spiritual help.

Some people end up taking medication to try and control the symptoms. While this can be a huge help in the short term, it does not heal the cause of the inner pain – but it can help people live with the pain until God brings healing to the inner being. As we saw earlier, David experienced inner sickness as a result of his own sin. So, one of the primary healing steps for our soul can be to humbly and honestly deal with our own sin in confession and repentance before God. He will then be able to make us truly clean (James 5:16).

But when our inner sickness is caused by what others have done to us, then God has provided another remedy – forgiveness. In the Lord's prayer Jesus urged us to always be forgiving of others. It's one of the most healing things we can ever do – and we'll be looking more closely at this in Chapter 4.

Sickness in Our Body

Most people will first associate the word 'sick' with sickness of the body. The body is a truly amazing machine, made up of hundreds of mutually dependent organs, all of which serve the good of the whole. When something goes wrong with any one of the body's operating systems or, for example, the body has been poisoned by something we have eaten or breathed in, or we catch a disease, we say that we are sick or ill.

Bodily sickness can have its roots in a variety of different sources. There are many diseases in the world which are carried by germs and viruses. And we can catch them. There isn't any human being who isn't vulnerable to catching a cold, getting measles, being bitten by a mosquito and catching malaria or any one of hundreds of other identifiable diseases which are, ultimately, a result of our living in a fallen world.

But, sometimes, the body displays symptoms and feels ill because it is responding to things that are out of order in our spirit and soul – and that can be because of things we have done or things others have done to us. When that happens it's vital that we identify what the real problem is as a preparation for healing prayer. We will make little progress by only praying for the symptoms, if the real problem lies elsewhere.

We can also have received an inborn vulnerability to a particular condition through our parenting Something that has come down the generation line because of what the Bible refers to as the *'sins of the fathers'* (Exodus 20:5). And we can also be suffering the long-term consequences of accidents and traumas that haven't been fully healed.

There are many possible sources of sickness in the body. But as a general rule, even when praying for physical things it is good spiritual practice to clear the ground of our lives, of anything which has its source in our spirit and soul, which may be at the root of physical sickness within.

In James 5:14-16, James urges those who are sick to call the elders together, confess their sins and be anointed with oil for healing. And in that respect, nothing has changed! Good practice then is still good practice today.

In Need of Deliverance

When Jesus healed people, He frequently did so by ordering an evil or unclean spirit (a demon) to come out of the person. For Jesus recognised that if the sickness was caused or sustained by the presence of a demon, the person could only be fully healed when the evil spirit had gone.

In Luke 13: 10-17 Jesus heals a woman whose spine was bent double. He says she had been bound by a spirit for eighteen years. First, he dealt with the spirit and then he laid his hands on her for physical healing. It was a two-stage process.

And, so it is today, if a person has an unclean spirit, then they are in need of deliverance as well as healing. We have seen many, many people healed in this way. We will be learning more about how Jesus sets the captives free in Chapter 6.

Being honest with God!

There is an old saying 'Honesty is the best policy'. While it is not Scripture, the essence of its meaning is very scriptural. Jesus said *"I am the truth"* (John 14:6). So, if we are followers of Him then it should be the objective of our life to always be truthful.

On many occasions, we have met people who had symptoms that made life difficult for them and naturally they wanted prayer for the healing of their symptoms. But when we started asking questions about things in their life that could be at the root of their symptoms, they have been very reluctant to answer, or have even refused. Their desire to cover things up, especially things that were embarrassing or shameful, was sometimes greater than their desire for truthfulness and healing.

So, now is the time to do some private business with God and give Him permission as you read this book, to remind you of all those things in your life which may still be lying hidden in darkness, which need to be brought into the light.

You may not yet be ready to talk about these things with someone else. But a simple and very profound way of beginning to face reality about every aspect of our lives is to write as much as you can remember down in a *"letter to God"*. Then as you work through the book, you will find God begins to deal with them one step at a time, as you journey with Him.

On the wall of our kitchen we have a picture of a basketful of eggs. Beneath the picture are these words: *"I put all my eggs in one basket, and gave the basket to God."* Oh, so simple, but oh so meaningful when we do it with all our heart. He is utterly trustworthy and however large or small the mess may be in our lives, He is up to the job and won't let us down!

God Loves Me as I Am –
learning to trust Him

However hard we may try, we cannot make ourselves more loveable to God! Our relationship with Him may be damaged as a result of our sin, but nothing we do can change the nature and character of God.

Sometimes people find it hard to grasp this truth and are frightened to be 100% honest – even with God! They fear that if they are totally truthful about themselves, somehow or other, God won't love them. They forget that Jesus lived and died for us while we were yet sinners (Romans 5:8). He didn't ask us to clean ourselves up first – for we are totally incapable of cleaning up the spiritual dirt and healing ourselves! This is a work of God's grace, love and mercy. We cannot make ourselves more loveable!

The fact is, God IS Love (1 John 4:8). He didn't decide to love anybody – for His whole nature is love – from beginning to end – from Alpha to Omega. And no matter what lies in our background, be it things we've suffered or things we've done wrong, He still loves us – and longs for us to come back to Him. He is not put off by our past – but He does want us to come to Him, and allow Him to change us from the inside out and give us back the future destiny that Satan would want to rob us of.

One of the most powerful stories Jesus told was that of the Prodigal Son – the son who went off with his share of his inheritance, wasted it on all the excesses of a sinful life and finished up feeding the pigs! (Luke 15:11-32). The Pharisees were probably wondering what sort of punishment Jesus would say his father was planning for his son. Would He say that the punishment should be according to the law, stoning to death? They weren't ready for the wonderful end to Jesus's story! When the father saw his son coming home, from a long way off, he lifted up his skirts and ran to welcome him home and hug him!

The father's rejoicing knew no bounds for he said, *"This my son was dead and is alive again"* (v.24) or *"this my son was lost and now he is found"*. And there was a mighty celebration. There are many wonderful lessons to be learnt from this most amazing of parables. All the son had to do was turn and go back to his father – and that's all we need to do as well. As soon as we turn towards him, the Father comes running towards us, arms wide open, to greet us, hug us and celebrate.

God Wants Us to Come to Him – Just As We Are!

Satan wants us to look at any mess there may be in our lives and think that, because of this, God wouldn't want to know us. He tries to convince us that we might as well stay where we are, where we feel more familiar with our circumstances. It's easy to forget that Satan's a master deceiver (John 8:44) and that he will do everything he possibly can to convince us that we are unlovable and God couldn't possibly want us or use us in His Kingdom.

No matter what sort of mess there may have been in our lives, there is absolutely nothing we can do to make ourselves more acceptable and more loveable to God! Jesus invites us to come to Him, simply as we are.

God is the only one who can clean up the mess, give us new hope and a fresh start. Little by little He will change us from the inside out – all He requires is our cooperation. He won't force Himself upon us, but when we choose to walk with Him, we can be absolutely sure that He will walk with us.

At each stage of our journey, we will be finding out fresh truths about God and fresh truths about ourselves. If we open the doors of our hearts from the inside, we can totally trust Him to come in and lovingly begin the work of restoration.

Remember Isaiah 61:1! He came to heal the broken-hearted and set the captives free, He came to comfort those who mourn, to give us a garment of praise and to make us into His oaks of righteousness. And that includes you!

A Prayer to Help You

Thank you, Lord, for creating me in Your image and likeness and for showing me how much you love me. As I begin this journey of discovery I pray that you will help me to trust You every step of the way. I don't want there to be anything which will stand in the way of me fulfilling your purposes for my life.

Thank you for showing me how the different areas of my created being could be in need of healing. Help me to identify those places which are out of order in my life, so that, with Your help, Godly order can be restored.

And I pray that You will help me to understand the truths that are contained in Your Word. And then apply the lessons I have learned in my life.

In Jesus' Name, Amen

CHAPTER 2

Who is God and Who am I?

Discovering God's foundations for the journey of your life!

Many people choose not to believe in God or follow Him because of their own limited understanding of who He is. The God they have rejected often bears no resemblance to what He is really like. So, they haven't rejected God at all, they've only rejected a false image – an image which really does need to be rejected because it is false! And many of the people who do truly believe in God can still have a distorted view of what He is really like, which makes it difficult for them to relate to and trust in Him.

Sometimes that distorted view of the nature of God comes from the way their parents behaved. God intended parents to model to their children what their heavenly Father is like. So, those children whose parents are distant from them can grow up to believe that God is distant and doesn't really care for them. Parents who are harsh or, even, cruel, can give children the impression that God is more like an old man in the sky with a big stick in His hands than a loving Father! And parents who spoil their children by giving them whatever they want, often as a means of keeping them quiet, can be giving their children the impression that God will give them whatever they want, irrespective of whether or not it's good for them!

So, an absolutely essential stepping stone on our journey of discovery of God's healing, is to lay aside all our pre-conceptions about who God is and what He is like and start to get to know Him as He really is. In Chapter 1 we began to understand something of how God made us, but now we need to go a little deeper into understanding the unique person that each of us is and how we can know and love ourselves.

There are lots of self-help courses out there, which offer all sorts of techniques to help you be master of your own self-improvement. Unfortunately, their value is severely limited by one unchangeable fact. Unless your world is illuminated by the Light of the World, you will always be living in spiritual darkness.

This means that you will have a distorted view of yourself and never reach a place of real peace and freedom, no matter how good the self-improvement course may be. This is because the Light of the World, Jesus, is the only One who can bring true light into our inner darkness and truly transform us into the person He made us to be. Only He has the blue-print for our lives.

There are many believers who would say they are thrilled that Jesus lived and died, so that their sins may be forgiven and they can go to Heaven. But when it comes to making Jesus Lord of their lives and living for Him here on Earth, they may not be quite so thrilled at the idea! But it is only when we choose to let Him be Lord of our lives that we can know the deepest healing and experience the greatest blessing – not just for today but throughout our lives.

In this Chapter we are aiming to put down a good foundation about both God and ourselves, so that we will have something solid to build on as we step forward into the future that He has prepared for us.

Who is God? Understanding the foundations of our faith

God is Creator

God is the Creator of all things – including mankind. We do not need to understand the detail of how He did it. Scientists have many different ways of describing the history of the Universe and the origin of life on Earth, but as Martin Rees, the *Astronomer Royal* and a former *President of the Royal Society* has said, science is no further forward in answering the question of what happened before the Universe came into being than St.Augustine in the fifth century!

The universe, the world and mankind are no accident. Everything speaks of there being a Creator. The psalmist expressed this so profoundly in Psalm 19:1-4 when he said: *"The heavens declare the glory of God; the skies proclaim the work of his hands. Day after day they pour forth speech; night after night they reveal knowledge. There is no speech or language where their voice is not heard. Their voice goes out into all the earth, their words to the end of the world."*

Paul expressed it this way in his letter to the Romans (1:20): *"For since the beginning of the world God's invisible qualities – his eternal power and divine nature – have been clearly seen, being understood from what has been made, so that men are without excuse."*

And then at the beginning of his Gospel John tells us what he had understood from all that Jesus had taught the disciples in those amazing three years of walking with Him: *"Through him all things were made, without him nothing was made that has been made"* (John 1:3).

I thank God that, even though I was trained as a scientist and am now a much older person, I have never lost the childhood wonder of what it was like to be wowed by God's creation. I can walk along the edge of a river and watch electric blue dragon flies glistening in the morning sun and shake my head in awe and wonder. I can see a pair of swans guarding their freshly hatched brood of cygnets and watch in amazement. Every walk becomes a litany of *"God, you're so clever!"* as my spirit rejoices in God my Saviour and the Creator of all things.

And at night I can join the psalmist and look up at the sky of miracles, rejoicing in the extraordinary genius that hung the stars in space. Then, as a scientist, I remember that if the value of gravity changed by an infinitesimally small amount (0.00000000000000001%) there would be no air to breathe and life would become impossible for mankind. I have learned to marvel at God's creative genius. His design for Planet Earth is beyond comparison or comprehension.

God is a Trinity of Father, Son and Holy Spirit

In the story of creation, we read that after creating the world God said, *"Let us make man in our image, in our likeness"* Genesis 1:26. The plural word 'us', declares that the oneness of God is comprised of more than one dimension.

Then Jesus, the Son of God, said that *"I and my Father are one"* (John 10:30). And it was this same Jesus who said to the disciples that after He returned to Heaven, *"I will ask the Father and, and he will give you another Counsellor – the Spirit of truth"* (John 14:16-17). And after Pentecost Peter confirmed that this had happened when he told the crowd in his sermon, that Jesus had *"received from the Father the promised Holy Spirit and poured out what you now see and hear"* (Acts 2:33).

While the word 'trinity' does not actually appear in the Scriptures, the fact of God being a Trinity of Father, Son and Holy Spirit is clearly evident throughout God's Word. We have a Father who loves us – He has a Son who died to save us and the Father sent the Holy Spirit to dwell within us and empower us.

The Names of God Reveal His Character

There are many different names of God revealed in the Scriptures. Each one tells us something about His nature and character. For example, He is described as Shepherd, Provider, Healer, Everlasting, Our Righteousness – and many, many more wonderful names. And Jesus also had two primary names. In the Old Testament He was prophesied to be *Emmanuel, or God with us* (Isaiah 7:14), a prophecy that was referred to in the New Testament in Matthew 1:23. But He was also to be called Yeshua, the Hebrew word for Jesus, as told to Mary by the angel Gabriel, *"You will be with child and will give birth to a son, and you are to give him the name, Jesus"* (Luke 1:31).

So, the very names of Jesus give us a vital understanding of who Jesus really was. The word Emmanuel tells us that He was sent by God to be with us on Earth, in order that He would become Yeshua, Jesus – meaning the one who would save us.

We also read in John 14:8-10 that Jesus came to show us what the Father is like. So, people cannot excuse themselves by saying *"we had no idea what God was like"* for, in Jesus we have a perfect representation of the nature of Father God. So, if we want to know what God is like then all we need to do is look at Jesus!

We have already established that God IS love – and that characteristic was shown to its fullest extent when Jesus chose to die on the cross, demonstrating both His and His Father's ultimate love for mankind, for you and for me. From the moment man first sinned, God's love motivated Him to mount a rescue plan for all those who would choose to come back to Him. *"For God so loved the world that he gave his one and only Son, that whoever believes in him shall not perish but have eternal life"* (John 3:16).

Because of the Fall, death is our inheritance. But unlike the rest of mankind, Jesus never sinned. Death, therefore, could have no power over Him. So, Jesus became the perfect sacrifice. Death was not his inheritance, but by choosing to die for us, He paid the full price of our sin and freed mankind from the consequences of having broken the law.

When we receive Jesus as our Saviour and are born again, it's as if we have already died, because Jesus died for us. And because He was raised from the dead, His resurrection life becomes ours also. This is the gift of salvation. In Scripture this is referred to as the New Covenant, through which we are able to receive forgiveness for our sins in time and know that because we are forgiven we will spend eternity with God in Heaven.

Right now, all those who know and love the Lord are waiting for Jesus to come again – this time He will return to reign as King.

Who am I? Understanding ME!

Scripture tells us that human beings are made in the image and likeness of God (Genesis 1:26). Jesus didn't have to change his appearance in order to come to Earth and look like a man, for God had already created mankind to have an appearance similar to Him – we are made in His image! But more than that, we are also created with similar characteristics. All human beings are created to both love and be loved and be creative – just like God!

If we want to understand how God feels about us, His children, all we have to do is ask how a mother or father feels towards their own precious children? Irrespective of whether or not they are believers they love their children unconditionally – even when they go astray, just as God still loves us. That love, in the heart, comes from God and is simply a reflection of the love there is in God's heart for us, His children, even though we have sinned against Him.

While we are all His children, we are all uniquely different and created by God with special characteristics, gifts and abilities. And each of us has a purpose to live for and a destiny to fulfil. Paul tells us in Ephesians 2:10 that we are *"created in Christ Jesus to do good works, which God prepared for us in advance."* The deepest joy any of us can experience in life is when we know that we are doing those things that God has made us for – His joy flows out from inside us. God rejoices when we become the person He made us to be.

Why do I need Jesus to help me?

Because of the Fall, when human beings chose to go their own way, we now live in a sinful world. And Satan, the god of this world, will always seek to undermine our walk of faith, or try to lead us into sin and rob us of our destiny. Satan truly is the enemy of souls.

Also, because of the Fall, we all have to wrestle with the reality of what we call a carnal, fleshly or sinful nature. Jeremiah even referred to the heart as being desperately wicked! (Jeremiah 17:9). The instinct of the sinful nature is always to respond to the temptations of the god of this world. It is at enmity with the Spirit of God.

So, the Christian walk can be a battle not to allow Satan, our enemy, score victories in our lives. Even the Apostle Paul struggled with temptation because of his own carnal nature. In Romans 7:14 to 20 he talks about how sometimes he has difficulty doing the good things he really wants to do and, at the same time, not doing the bad things that tempt his selfish carnal nature! No wonder Paul had to tell the Ephesians about the need to keep their spiritual armour on and take a stand against the devil's evil schemes (Ephesians 6:10-18). There is a battle going on for our soul and for our destiny.

Sometimes Jesus is described as the *second Adam*. Jesus was conceived in the womb of Mary by the Holy Spirit and, like Adam, He was without sin. But the difference between the first Adam and Jesus was that, unlike Adam, He never succumbed to temptation and He remained without sin. Sin separated man from God so that our eternal destiny became the same as that of Satan – eternal death (Romans 6:23). Following our physical death, therefore, there would be a spiritual death causing us to be separated from God for eternity in what the Bible refers to as Hell (Matthew 25:41).

But, because Jesus never sinned, when He died, death had no hold over Him and on resurrection morning there was a mighty victory over Satan. And the wonderful news is, those who believe in Jesus are in Him – which means the death Jesus died as the price for sin becomes ours. And His resurrection life becomes ours also.

This is why the term being born again so precisely describes the real Christian life. Just as Jesus is alive for evermore, all those who trust in Jesus will also be alive with Him for evermore. Those who are born again have a new life in Christ and our eternity is secure because we are in Him.

John Newton expressed these wonderful truths so power-fully in his hymn *Amazing Grace*:

> *Amazing Grace!*
> *How sweet the sound*
> *That saved a wretch like me*
> *I once was lost but now am found*
> *Was blind but now I see.*

But, even those who are born again, will still have to face temptations, through which Satan tries to lead us into sin and rob us of our destiny. Only Jesus has overcome Satan. It is only He, therefore, by the enabling power of Holy Spirit, who can help us day by day to overcome our own temptations. Jesus died that we might be forgiven and so that we might be healed and restored and continue being blessed doing those things that He has made us for. We need His presence and strength inside us.

Making Jesus Lord

So, Jesus is not only the Son of God, who became the Saviour of the world, but also the One who, as Lord of our lives, gives us access to all the blessings of our spiritual inheritance. For, as John tells us, *"all who received him, to those who believed in his name, he gave the right to become children of God – children born not of natural descent, nor of human decision nor a husband's will, but born of God"*

(John 1:12-13). As believers in Him we are incredibly privileged to know and love the one who is also King of Kings, and Lord of Lords – He is Lord over all!

Sadly, there are many Christians who only want Jesus to be their Saviour, because they are aware of their sin and want to have eternal life. But they don't want to live their lives on Earth under the Lordship of Jesus, with Him providing the motivation of their heart. They want to have a foot in both worlds – the world of truth and life and the world of sinfulness, selfishness and death.

Only God knows the true state of each person's heart, but one thing we have observed many times over the years is *that choosing to live our Christian life with Jesus as Lord of All is one of the most important keys to healing.* Only then will we want to put right those things in our lives which grieve our heavenly Father. And only then will we see the hand of God's blessing bringing wholeness and restoration into each and every area of our lives.

Jesus died as our Saviour, but He rose from the dead as Lord over ALL, including Satan, death and hell. So, when we accept Him as Saviour and make Him Lord of our lives, we enter into His victory on the cross for us. When we submit our lives to His Lordship and His direction for our lives, we are then on track towards the place of His blessing, fulfilling His purposes for our lives. This is a vital step on our journey of healing. At this point we discover that for Jesus to be Lord of our lives means that we are swimming against the current of this world – and that's not easy. But great joy and blessing can come into our lives as a result –

This would be a good moment on our journey of discovery, therefore, to come afresh to Jesus and invite Him not only to be our Saviour, but also to be the Lord of every area of our being.

Here's a Prayer You Could Pray if You Are Ready to Take This Vital Step:

Thank You, Jesus, that even though you had never sinned, you chose to die on the cross for me, that I might be forgiven and receive new life. I confess that I am a sinner in need of a Saviour and I invite you, Jesus, to come into my life to be my Saviour and my Lord.

I come to you, Lord, just as I am, with all the issues and problems of my life. I choose to lay them at the foot of the cross and ask you to help me, as I receive forgiveness for my sins and choose to give You first place in every area of my life, and on each step of life's journey.

I invite you to be Lord of my spirit and my relationship with Father God; Lord of my mind and all my thoughts; Lord of my emotions and all my reactions; Lord of my will and all my decisions; Lord of my body and all my behaviour; Lord of my past, my present and my future.

I invite you to reign in every area of my life and to show me those places where I am in need of Your healing. And I pray, Lord, that You will restore in me Your purposes and destiny for my life. Thank You Lord for everything You are and all that You've done for me. Amen.

CHAPTER 3

Rebuilding Life – God's Way

Discovering the God who loves and heals

His way or my way?

Having taken the step of making Jesus Lord of our lives, we can now start to look at the consequences of choosing to follow Him in all things.

I have learnt a little about human nature down the years, so I wasn't surprised to hear that the most-popular and most-sung song throughout the whole of the twentieth century, was Frank Sinatra's *"I did it my way"*. But few people realise that the lyrics of this still popular song are all about the end of life and what a person might say to God after going through the final curtain of death!

The first verse says:

And now, the end is near
And so I face the final curtain
My friend, I'll say it clear
I'll state my case, of which I'm certain.

I've lived a life that's full
I've travelled each and every highway
But more, much more than this
I did it my way.

Then in the last verse the words make fun of someone who prays to God *(one who kneels)*, without any concern for the consequence of man's supreme arrogance in being proud of his pride, and telling God that there may have been a right way, but mine wasn't a wrong way, I just did it my way!

For what is a man, what has he got
If not himself, then he has naught
To say the things he truly feels
And not the words of one who kneels
The record shows I took the blows
And did it my way
Yes, it was my way

Sadly, this is not only a prevailing attitude among most people in the twenty-first century. It is an attitude that can also be evident in the church. Some Christians, and even some churches, have begun to modify their moral code to fit in with what the world does, rather than standing firm on what God has said in His Word. Jesus urged us to be *'salt and light'* in the world, not to bring the world into the church!

In our pursuit of the way to wholeness and freedom we will inevitably discover that the more a person has tried to do things 'my way', the less whole they actually are! Scripture tells us that *"there is a way that seems right to a man, but its end is the way to death."* (Proverbs 16:25).

In my College teaching days, I made something of a speciality of studying building defects and showing students what would happen if things had not been done in the right way. Sometimes, buildings had to be pulled down because they hadn't been constructed properly from the foundations up. In effect, such buildings were not able to fulfil their purpose or, more simply they had 'died'!

Many times, I have had to help people see that some of the problems they were facing had their origins in *"do it my way"* decisions. When living their lives outside the plans and purposes of God, things had gone badly wrong. Their lives were like a building that had been built on a poor foundation or with unsound building materials. They had been building in their own way – but it wasn't God's way – and the building of their life was in danger of collapse.

We can all be guilty of trying to 'do it my way' at various stages of our life. Most times we are not aware of the connection between current issues and things we did, or which happened to us a long time ago. But God knows, and from many years of experience, seeing Him help thousands of people, I know that He longs to help you as well, even when there have been times when you have chosen to do things your way instead of His!

You may not feel right now that you have any major problems, but sometimes people say things like this, *"When I faced all the things that could be wrong and let God change me from the inside out, it felt as though I had moved out from the slow lane and really started to live."*

So, may I encourage you at this critical stage of our journey of discovery to take your hands off the controls and let God do things His way – it's always the best way!

When we hand over the controls of our life to God, He rejoices to help us put things right. He doesn't destroy us because we've got some things wrong, but helps us see what mistakes we may have made. He then shows us how to start again and rebuild our lives on a new foundation. And when it comes to that life-rebuild *"no-one can lay any foundation other than the one already laid, which is Jesus Christ"* (1Cor. 3:11). Jesus is the one and only foundation that will never fail.

We have a derelict chapel in the grounds of Ellel Grange and we needed a professional surveyor to do a report on everything that needs to be done to bring the building back into use. In just the same way, we need God to survey the building that is our life to date. For this is what we are offering Him, when we make Him Lord of our lives.

Living life God's way doesn't mean that things are stripped away from us ruthlessly. God always gives us the time we need, and when the time is right He helps us by the enabling power of His Holy Spirit. So, let's not hang on to things which we know are wrong, trying to do things *'my way'*! And then we will need His help to restore those things that need to be rebuilt in His way, rather than ours.

A song that used to be popular, and which spoke powerfully to me many years ago and which I pray will be a living testimony for those who are *Discovering Wholeness*, has these words:

> *"Something beautiful, something good,*
> *All my confusion He understood,*
> *All I had to offer Him was brokenness and strife,*
> *But He made something beautiful, of my life"*
>   (Bill Gaither)

Those words express the wonderful truth that Jesus came to heal the broken-hearted, comfort those who mourn and set the captives free – including you and me!

In order to live life God's way, we need to understand from God's Word the divine protocol of how He wants to help us through the work of His Spirit. God only has good for us, so we have nothing to fear. He will never give us second best. No matter how messed up our life might have become, we can totally trust Him to lead us into His purposes for our lives – doing those things that we were made for and experiencing His joy at the very heart of our being.

Giving everything to God – the good the bad and the ugly!

A very important step in making Jesus Lord of our lives is to consciously lay everything in our lives before Him. There can be nothing we try to hide from Him.

A large house has many rooms. When guests come, the owner of the house might choose which rooms he is happy for people to see. The doors of all the other rooms are kept firmly shut! Our lives, too, can be like a large house. There can be many rooms and we don't want people to know what lies behind some of the doors! Those things may be embarrassing, or painful and we don't want to face them again ourselves and we definitely don't want anyone else to see the reality of what we have done in our personal history.

But often, it is the things that lie behind those doors that are the cause of symptoms we may be struggling with – but the freedom and healing won't come unless we give God permission to deal with the hidden issues which are at the root of unwholeness in our lives. I will never forget the lady who endured painful physical symptoms for sixteen years – until she confessed she was injured in an accident when she was on her way to commit adultery!

For some, choosing to face the truth about themselves and give everything to God – the good, the bad and the ugly – is a major challenge. They may feel that if they bring all those things into the light of God's truth, that He will no longer love them! They forget that God is omniscient – which means He already knows everything!

Nothing can be hidden from Him. He's not sitting on the edge of His throne waiting to find out what's behind those doors! He already knows what's there and it hasn't stopped Him loving anyone yet! But He won't over-ride the free will that He gave to all human beings. So, He waits for us to bring those things to Him.

You have absolutely nothing to fear from God. You can totally trust Him. If we try and keep back part of our lives from Him, we will only be depriving ourselves of the blessing that God would want us to have and to enjoy.

Satan will encourage us not to let God have access to certain areas of our lives – especially those which contain what I call the 'comfort or embarrassing sins' – the things we are tempted to run back to when we are struggling or going through a difficult time. Things like alcohol, cigarettes, excess food, chocolate, drugs, ungodly sexual relationships, pornography etc. The more honest and open we are with God the greater will be the fullness of His love and blessing. As Jesus said in Luke 7:47 – those who are forgiven much, love much!

One of Satan's favourite questions is to ask how we will cope if we don't have those things to fall back on?! The answer lies in a deeper, renewed relationship with God who becomes very real and our ultimate source of comfort in all circumstances. Paul tells us in 2 Corinthians 1:3 that our heavenly Father is *"the God of all comfort."* It is to Him that we must learn to run in time of need.

And please don't believe the other lie of Satan, that God doesn't love you because of whatever you are ashamed of or embarrassed by. The truth is He couldn't love you any more just as you are, even with these things! But He also loves you enough to want you to be free from their bondage. He doesn't want us to stay that way.

Whenever we hang onto anything negative, we rob our future lives of positive blessings. And if we don't let Him have what you might describe as the bad and the ugly, then He can't heal and restore us! In truth, it is the bad and the ugly He most wants us to acknowledge and release to Him for healing, because He knows how much these things rob us of real life. God won't reject you if you're honest – He already knows the worst about you and still loves you!

Discovering God's order for mankind

In the last chapter, we saw that both God and humans are three-in-one. God is Father, Son and Holy Spirit, and human beings are spirit, soul and body. When Jesus was talking to a woman He met at Jacob's well, in John 4, He told her that God is Spirit – and that those who worship Him must worship Him in spirit and in truth (John 4:24).

God gave us a human spirit so that we may enjoy the deepest level of fellowship and relationship with Him. This is the heart of worship – fellowshipping with Father God. We don't have to be singing to worship God, although sometimes we experience deep levels of intimacy with God when we are expressing our love for Him in song. I've learnt over the years that every moment of every day can be an opportunity for worship as we thank God for His blessings or look at His creation.

When we worship, we open up our own hearts to God's Holy Spirit. Worship and the indwelling of His Spirit go hand in hand. When we are doing those things that please God we are worshipping God, but when we are doing those things that please Satan (rebellion against God) we are also worshipping, but now we are surrendering ourselves to the god of this world. And we don't receive Holy Spirit from this kind of worship but we do make ourselves vulnerable to the influence and possible indwelling, of an unclean, or evil spirit. That is one of the reasons, for example, why people who have consciously chosen to sin, then sometimes feel unable to resist similar temptations in the future – they have given an unclean spirit the authority to have influence over them. In Chapter 6 we will look more closely at this problem and how to be set free.

We don't always feel like worshipping God, though, especially if something has become a barrier between us and Him. On occasions, God used David's spirit to speak to his soul in order to bring it into line with his inner desire to worship and follow God (Psalm 103). His flesh, and the will of his soul, sometimes got in the way of his spirit!

God's original order for mankind was that we should have a spiritual relationship with Him and that our soul (mind, emotions and will) and our body should come under the headship of our spirit. That means that if our soul takes its instructions from the redeemed spirit, that the body, would then only do those things that please God. Both our spirit and our soul can operate as if they have a will of their own. And sometimes, if our spirit has been crushed or broken, it may struggle to respond to God and act in cooperation with His Holy Spirit.

When humanity first sinned in the Garden of Eden, it was the desires of the flesh (for the beautiful fruit that had been forbidden) which over-rode the will of the spirit. God's order was reversed, and sin was the result. This is the constant battle that every Christian faces on a daily basis – not to let the will of the flesh over-ride the will of the spirit.

When we talk about 'the flesh' we are not just referring to a sinful tendency of the body – but to the combination of the soul and the body, working together in harmony. The body never sins of its own accord – the sins of the flesh happen when the soul uses the body to fulfil sinful desires.

The whole journey of discipleship (the application of personal discipline to see God's order established and His will done in one's life) is about living the Christian life under the Lordship of Jesus. This means that the activities of our soul and our body are submitted to the will of God, communicated by Him through His Word and via the Spirit.

The Scriptures are a divine workshop manual to instruct us in the ways of the Lord. It is as we read the Word of God that the Holy Spirit, who inspired what was written, speaks into our lives, leads and directs our steps. It's important to take something in of the Word of God on a daily basis, just as we would read a daily newspaper. We read the newspaper so as to keep up to date with what is happening in the world. And we read the Scriptures daily so God can keep us up to date with what He wants to teach us and speak into our lives. It is through reading His Word that God writes truth on our hearts and transforms our mind and our thinking.

I will be eternally grateful for parents who encouraged me to read a small portion of Scripture every day, followed by the daily *Scripture Union* bible-reading notes appropriate for my age. I read something from the Word of God every day and even now, seventy years later, I am still blessed by the things I took in as a child, which the Holy Spirit can remind me of as and when necessary.

Choosing to live my life God's way

When a person is born again, their renewed spirit becomes alive to God. As born-again people, the Holy Spirit can then renew our conscience so that we are restored to have a finely-tuned God-sensitivity. This then becomes an indicator of God's guiding hand on our life and the way He wants us to go.

Little by little, one day at a time, we take on more and more of the God-likeness with which God first created mankind (2 Corinthians 3:18). The early church fathers used to call that process 'sanctification', or growing to be more like Jesus in the way we think, the way we speak and what we do with our lives.

While we can now see everything from a God-inspired perspective, there can still be a lot of work to be done to re-orient our lives. We may now, because we are believers, be walking in a different direction, but salvation doesn't change our history! And throughout that history we have grown used to ungodly thinking and doing things in an ungodly way which has left deep ruts in the pathway of our life. It takes time to re-orient our lives and walk away from our past, so that we say 'no' to sinful choices and consistently walk in the ways of the Spirit.

Satan will still tempt us to fall back into the old ways of thinking and living, and because we found them comfortable in the past, we may begin to crave the comfort of the old ways. But God knows that, and so He put it into His Word that *"If we confess our sins, he is faithful and just and will forgive us and cleanse us from all unrighteousness"* (1 John 1:9). Unrighteousness means those things in our lives which God cannot bless.

If we do slip up on life's journey, then it is vital that we keep short accounts with God. This means dealing with those things with Him, just as soon as we are aware of what went wrong. This is an important foundational principle of discipleship and the sooner we come back to God in repentance, the sooner we will be able to get up again and move on in our Christian walk.

As well as learning to walk through life in God's way, we now need to start asking God to show us any wrong directions we have taken in the past and any new directions He wants us to take now. Prior to becoming a Christian, we made decisions without involving God in the process, and even as Christians we might have continued to do that on occasions. So, we may have made a lot of wrong choices which God will want to help us resolve so we can get back on the right pathway.

Learning to live life God's way involves listening to God and asking Him to show us the direction He now wants us to go – and the things that He would want to change. For some this could even mean a complete restructuring of life as God gives fresh vision for the future.

The years ahead could be the most exciting and fruitful of your whole life, as you watch God's hand at work reorienting everything. It's like asking God to put His hands over yours as you turn the steering wheel of your life, so that His hand becomes the guiding hand, keeping your life on track. In the past the enemy may have been turning the steering wheel and driving your life in wrong directions.

Welcoming Change – Even When it's Hard

When we have grown comfortable with the old ways, we can have a built-in resistance to change. It's hard to re-programme our on-board computer!

Sanctification may be an old word, but it accurately describes the process. It simply means overcoming by the power of the Holy Spirit the ways of the sinful nature, living according to the Spirit and becoming more like Jesus. Much of Paul's writings are aimed at helping Christians do just that – especially in the letters he wrote to the Galatians, the Ephesians, the Philippians and to Timothy. These letters are full of practical guidelines for godly living – and also some important warnings of how wrong things can get, if we choose to live life 'our way' instead of 'God's way'.

For example, in Philippians 4:8 Paul advises us to adjust how we think – because every action we do begins first as a thought. If we dwell on it, it can then become a desire and finally the desire becomes a decision which our body carries out!

Paul encourages us to ask God to help us think about those things that are pleasing to Him –*"whatever is true, whatever is noble, whatever is right, whatever is pure, whatever is lovely, whatever is admirable – if anything is excellent or praiseworthy – think on these things."*

What we think eventually determines what we do and what we become. So, if we think on things like the above our actions will become more godly, and we will grow to be more like Him. But no-one can pretend that at times it isn't hard and that it doesn't feel like an uphill battle. But the rewards are sweet, the blessings are rich. The more we welcome changes that are inspired by God's Spirit – the more we will enter into the destiny He has prepared for us.

A Prayer to Help You

*Thank You, Lord, that Your love for me is unconditional.
I confess that there have been times in my life when I
have chosen to "do it my way" instead of Your way and
I ask you to forgive me for my arrogance and pride.*

*I pray that You will help me identify those times and
seasons when I have gone off-track. I then ask that You
will show me what their consequences have been, how
to undo the past and live with You at the centre of my
life in the future.*

*I choose, today, to be open to change. I want to be
transparent before You and I invite You into every room
of the house of my life, no matter what may lie behind
closed doors. I am intent, Lord, on bringing my life into
godly order and I am looking forward to discovering
the wholeness and freedom that you have for me in all
the years that lie ahead. In Jesus' Name, Amen.*

CHAPTER 4

Forgive and be Forgiven

Discovering the joy of forgiveness

Unforgiveness is one of the most dangerous 'diseases' to afflict mankind! It cuts right through to the core of who we are and unless treated can give rise to a myriad of hurtful, painful, damaging and, even, lethal symptoms! So, in this chapter we need to be asking the Lord to help us not to leave any *'unforgiveness stone'* unturned, for hiding beneath some of those stones can be some of the most poisonous episodes of our lives, festering and still affecting our lives today.

The subject of forgiveness was so important to Jesus that when He gave the disciples a pattern for their prayer life (*what we call the Lord's Prayer in Matthew 6:9-13*), at its heart were words of confession (*forgive us our trespasses*) and words of release to others who have hurt us (*as we forgive those who have trespassed against us*).

This was clearly of great importance to Jesus for He then told the disciples that if they did not forgive others for what they had done, then His Father in Heaven would not be able to forgive them (Matthew 9:15). And that's pretty serious stuff.

None of us would want to think that we can't be forgiven for the things we have done. But it's clear from Scripture that if we don't deal with our sin then there will be consequences. Remember what Jesus said to the paralysed man He had just healed, *"Sin no more that nothing worse may happen to you"* (John 5:14). And James emphasised this principle when he was giving instructions in his letter about praying for healing (James 5:16). He encouraged the one who was asking for prayer to confess their sins, before being anointed with oil for healing.

Many years ago God gave us a pattern for our *Healing Retreats,* which included four different aspects of forgiveness. When we put these into practice we were amazed to discover just how much healing flows from God into our lives when we deal with our pride, face the issues head on and move forward into a new era of wholeness, freedom and hope.

It's so easy for people to think that you can just forget the past and move on, without dealing with the circumstances which have given rise to unforgiveness. We are all very good at putting a layer of impermeable spiritual concrete over such things and pretending that they no longer affect us today! Nothing could be further from the truth. For, what we bury unhealed festers in the background and can cause deep-seated spiritual, emotional, psychological, physical and, even, psychiatric problems, sometimes, even, causing people to feel suicidal.

Psalm 51 is a diary of King David's journey of healing when he had to face the sinful reality of his adultery with Bathsheba, and subsequent murder of her husband, Uriah. In respect of his relationship with God, this was David's darkest hour. So many of the words of this psalm are expressions of his need for forgiveness and healing at the very deepest level:

"have mercy on me, O God . . . blot out my transgressions . . .

cleanse me from my sin . . . my sin is ever before me . . . against you and you only have I sinned and done evil in your sight . . . wash me and I shall be whiter than snow . . . hide your face from my sins and blot out all my iniquities . . . take not your Holy Spirit from me . . . restore to me the joy of my salvation . . . the sacrifices of God are a broken spirit, a broken and a contrite heart, O God, you will not despise."

In verse 6, David says *"Behold, you delight in truth in the inward being."* Yes, even in those hidden parts which we have long-since buried, or rooms in our life containing personal secrets which lie hidden behind closed and locked doors. God is wanting to heal us and set us free from all these things – just as David was forgiven and healed following confession and repentance of his own sin.

So, to ensure that nothing gets left behind on our journey of discovery, we must look very carefully, one by one, at those four vital areas of forgiveness which have been central to the teaching on thousands of Ellel Ministries *Healing Retreats,* all over the world. You will find even more about this in my book *Forgiveness – God's Master Key,* also published by Sovereign World.

Getting my Slate Clean

I'm old enough to remember using a slate and chalk at my first school, instead of paper and pencil or pen! At the end of each day the teacher had to wipe all the slates clean, so we could have a fresh start with our spellings or our sums the next morning! Without a clean slate the following day's writing would be confusing and may not make any sense.

In a similar way, if we leave behind unconfessed and, therefore, unforgiven sins, the next stages of our lives are influenced, sometimes radically, by the things that lie partly hidden beneath the succeeding layers of life. We may then have difficulty in making sense of what is going on and the problems we encounter!

Pride is the biggest obstacle to overcome when dealing with the past and Satan uses this to try and keep those hidden things unresolved. For, as long as they remain unforgiven they have power to influence our future, and Satan can continue to use them against us.

Confessing sin is more than just telling God what we've done wrong. The word 'confess' means to agree with what God thinks about the sin. We can't make excuses or disagree with what God says – if God has said something is sinful, then it is! Sin is defined as rebellion against God (1 John 3:4). Sin is also sometimes described as 'missing the mark'. After sin has been truly confessed and forgiven, there can then be a full restoration of relationship with God and healing from the consequences of our sin can begin (1 John 1:9; Proverbs 28:13).

We have found it helpful to encourage people to take a little time looking at anything that might be left on the 'slate' of their lives. So, I would encourage you to identify all those things that you have done that you shouldn't have done, and all those things you didn't do which you know you should have done.

Write them down on a piece of paper so that when you come to pray you won't forget anything. Then bring each one of those situations to God, asking Him to forgive and to cleanse (1 John 1:9) and to heal (James 5:16) and to create in you a clean heart and renew a right spirit within you (Psalm 51:10).

I was teaching on this one day when, after the meeting, a lady came up to me under great conviction and obviously very distressed. She poured out that she had a responsible job as the office manager in the place where she worked, and always went above and beyond what was asked of her by her boss. In her job she also had responsibility for the firm's petty cash account and told me that for the previous twenty years she had always taken something for herself out of the petty cash every week because, she thought, she deserved it for all her hard work.

She had deceived herself into believing that this was OK. But this had now become a huge item on her personal slate, amounting to many thousands of pounds which had been stolen from her employers. No wonder that over the years she had lost her peace and joy and felt distant from God! The simple act of confession of what she had done gave her the confidence to face the issue with her employer and bring her life back into godly order.

Another lady came with her husband for prayer because they were having difficulty conceiving a child. I felt prompted to ask if she had ever had an abortion. She was obviously shocked by my question. For, the fact that she had fallen pregnant by another man as a teenager and her parents had helped her get an abortion, was a very dark secret which no-one else knew about. But having an abortion is taking the life of another human being, a serious sin that was still on her slate. She was able to bring it out into the open and receive God's forgiveness. Her husband forgave her for never having told him and, amazingly, once she had been delivered of the spirit of death from her womb she was very soon able to conceive.

These are just two examples of the healing principle expressed by James 5:16 which urges believers to confess their sins as part of their healing journey.

Forgiving me!

We've all done things that later we came to regret, and when it comes to facing the consequential issues we can be very hard on ourselves! If, as a result of our actions, something bad happened we may be tempted to say, *"I'll never forgive myself for . . . . . ."* And years later we are still bound by our own words as the regrets of the past repeatedly haunt us in the present.

Words such as these can tie us into unpleasant consequences that restrict our freedom. They can act like a curse on our lives and keep us in bondage to the past. They give the enemy power to hold us into the original incident and consequences of whatever it was we did that was so awful.

This is especially relevant when someone causes an accident that could have been avoided, which may have injured another person, or made a huge mistake in respect of a relationship, their finances or, perhaps, their career.

God does not want us to be held back by refusing to forgive ourselves. If God is willing to forgive us and wipe the slate clean, then by not forgiving ourselves we are saying that what Jesus did on the cross for us isn't good enough!

So, however bad such issues may have been in your own life, God wants you to thank Him for His forgiveness for what you did and then forgive yourself. Sometimes there can be real inner brokenness at the time when something bad happens and we need to ask God to do what Isaiah promised Jesus would do – heal the broken-hearted – and set the captives free (Isaiah 61:1). We will be looking more carefully at this issue of brokenness in Chapter 8.

Forgiving others

Most believers know that the things we do wrong are sinful. But few realise that holding other people in unforgiveness is also sinful and prevents us from being able to receive God's forgiveness for the things we have done (Matthew 6:15). We have seen how people with an unforgiving and bitter disposition are more likely to suffer from certain physical conditions. Unforgiveness is not only a major obstacle to receiving God's healing, but can also be the root cause of some medical problems.

We may think in terms of our body being functionally separated from our inner being. But that isn't the case. Even though there are three different dimensions to our humanity (spirit, soul and body), we are still one person and what affects one part can also have the capacity to have damaging consequences in another. It is not unusual for people to develop psychological, and even physical, problems as a result of the inner distress caused by unforgiveness and the pain of bitterness.

When people say things like *"I'll never forgive . . . (someone) for what they have done"*, they are actually condemning themselves to suffer the consequences of an ungodly choice. How can we ask God to forgive us for other things, if we are refusing to offer the same forgiveness to others?

One of the most significant healing steps we can take is to spend some time with the Lord, praying through our lives and asking Him to remind us of all those down the years who have hurt us in various ways, and speaking out our forgiveness. It is helpful to be clear about the way in which we have been hurt by their actions. You can use words like these for each one: *"I forgive you (name), for (what they did) and I release you into the freedom of my forgiveness."*

After each named person that you forgive, pray that God will heal you of anything which has come into your life as a result of being unforgiving or bitter. And if there are people on your list whose names you can't remember, but you can't remember their name, just tell God about that person and what happened, and forgive them anyway.

Where you have been very hurt by someone, there may be a lot of pain associated with what happened. In these cases, you may need to forgive on several occasions over a period of time. On each occasion, you will touch deeper levels of pain which you had previously covered up in order to try and get on with life. In these cases, you will need to keep on forgiving until all the pain has been given to Jesus and the pain no longer has power over you.

In Matthew 18 we read how Simon Peter asked Jesus how often he needed to forgive someone. He asked if seven times was enough! He must have been very surprised by Jesus' reply – *seventy times seven* (Matthew 18:21-22). And while the arithmetic says that this means 490, in reality it is a Jewish phrase which actually means *'don't even count'*. So, Jesus was saying there is no limit to the number of times you may have to forgive someone – and if there was a limit, then we would have to face the grim prospect of there being a limit on the number of times God is willing to forgive us.

Sometimes people feel that they can't forgive unless the other person says sorry. That is understandable – but wrong. For in most cases that will never happen and then we would be condemned for evermore! Another person's sin is their responsibility – our choice to forgive is our responsibility. By forgiving we are not saying that what someone did is now OK or didn't matter, we are simply cutting ourselves off from the consequences of unforgiveness and, even, bitterness in our own heart and trusting the other person to God.

Forgiving others is a true master key to healing – for unforgiveness can affect so many different areas of our lives. One man I knew was very reluctant to start the process, not being convinced that it would make any difference. But he chose to do so, nevertheless. A little while later he came and asked for help to find more people he could forgive, such was the release and joyful blessing he was now experiencing!

In ongoing life, there are all sorts of ways in which we can be hurt. So, it is a good personal discipline to regularly ask the Lord to help us keep our personal forgiveness of others up to date!

'Forgiving' God

God is Holy! Therefore, there are no wrong motives in His heart, no ungodly actions and no sin! But sometimes we blame God for things that have happened as if He was the cause of bad things that happened to us.

We need to say sorry to God for holding Him responsible for bad things, as if He had done them! Or, sometimes, He didn't stop bad things happening. In reality, all these things are the consequence of the Fall (man's choice to obey Satan and disobey God).

We may need to say sorry, too, for blaming God for not protecting us from even our own mistakes or disasters, such as accidents or acts of terror, caused by the wrong-doing or carelessness of others. We need to remember that God gave all of us the gift of freewill choice and, no matter what the circumstances, He does not rescind a gift He has given.

None of us are exempt from the possibility of suffering in this fallen world. How we react to those difficult things we experience will determine how well we recover from the consequences.

If we have a seed of unforgiveness, judgement or bitterness in our heart against God Himself, it may give rise to other roots of bitterness growing up and producing bad fruit in different areas of our lives.

In Conclusion

When people have faced and dealt with all four different areas of forgiveness, they are then in a good place to move on in life with God, discovering His wholeness and trusting Him to direct and lead them through all the issues of life. Spending time dealing with the past creates a solid foundation on which to build a new future with God, trusting Him for every step of the way ahead. And, as the old chorus says:

"My Lord knows the way through the wilderness,
All I have to do is to follow!"

A Prayer to Help You

I am sorry, Lord, for the things I have done which have grieved You. But I am so very grateful that Your Word teaches that when I confess my sins before You, and turn from them, that You have promised to forgive me and to cleanse me from all unrighteousness.

I know I can't change my history, but I do now choose to forgive myself for all those things that I have regretted and which have hurt me or others. I don't want to remain in bondage to any of those things and choose to accept Your freedom.

And, Lord, I know there are people who have hurt me in my past. Right now I choose to forgive them all, whatever it is they have done, and release them into the freedom of my forgiveness. I don't want to live even one more day nurturing bitterness or unforgiveness in my heart.

And finally, Lord, I'm sorry if I have ever blamed you for things that have gone wrong – for things that were my or other people's fault. Please forgive me.

And as I take these huge steps towards Your order being established in my life I pray that You will do a deep work of healing in me, and begin to restore me according to Your plans and purposes. I want to trust You for each and every step of the way ahead. In Jesus' name, Amen

CHAPTER 5

Rejected No More

Discovering God's unconditional love

We were created by God for relationship – firstly with Him and then with each other. Because relationships are absolutely central to our humanity, rejection is one of the most painful and deep-seated emotions that we can ever experience. It is one of the most powerful curses that can ever affect a human being.

Rejection touches right down into the very core of our humanity, deeply affecting the human spirit and, at its worst, it has the potential to render people unable to function at anything more than a superficial level. It can leave them unable to live up to their potential or walk in their personal destiny. This is a really important issue for us to understand and to discover how God wants to heal those who have been hurt most through rejection.

No matter how deep, how personal or, even, how cruel someone's experience of rejection may have been, there is no rejection that can ever be experienced that is greater than what Jesus must have felt on the cross. Here, the totally sinless Son of God was being publicly executed in open, unrestricted view, in a final act of absolute and cruel rejection of everything He is and everything He came to do. Isaiah summed this up prophetically when he said: *"He was despised and rejected by mankind, a man of suffering, and familiar with pain"* (Isaiah 53:3). Of one thing we can be absolutely certain, Jesus understands rejection.

It is recorded in John 3:16 that *"God so loved the world that He gave His only Son that whoever believes in Him should not perish but have eternal life."* This was the gift that God sent to mankind from the courts of Heaven and which mankind chose to reject. The very people whom Jesus came to save were nailing Him to a cross. And even as they did so Jesus was saying, *"Father forgive them, they do not know what they are doing"* (Luke 23:34). Jesus was not going to let any unforgiveness or bitterness of heart taint the dying moments of his life through being trapped into a sinful response.

Satan and the powers of darkness had done their worst, but there was no stain of sin on the heart of Jesus as He died. The triumph of resurrection morning was imminent – when the Lord Jesus Christ would rise, with his arms outstretched towards sinful man in a healing embrace of love, the ultimate remedy for the curse of rejection. The One who had said *"Come unto me all you who are heavy laden"* while on Earth (Matthew 11:28) – is still saying it to all who would look to Him. For He is the ultimate remedy for the broken heart and rejected spirit of every human being.

Jesus put no conditions on His invitation to come to Him and no-one was excluded. By example He was content to minister to the bottom end of society (the prostitutes and 'sinners') and told the story of the prodigal son, in which the Father welcomes back the one who has been wasting his life in 'a far country' (Luke 15:11-32).

In order to experience the healing that God has prepared for us from any form of rejection there are some primary truths that we need to embrace.

Accepting God – as He is!

Firstly, we need to accept and trust God as He really is – that means not believing in a distorted version of His true nature and character.

We have already understood that God is the Creator of all things – the universe and everything in it has its origin in God. The Bible declares that in the beginning God created the heavens and the earth. The idea that the trillions of tons of matter that form the universe and the trillions of stars that populate space could accidentally create themselves out of nothing is beyond reason. There are more stars in the universe than there are grains of sand on the whole of Planet Earth! Creator God has revealed Himself, His nature and His character through His creation (Romans 1:20)

We have also recognised that God is Love. God did not choose to love us – He IS love. Love is His very nature. We never need to doubt that God loves every human being. Nobody is beyond the capacity of God to love, nor has anyone done something so terribly awful that when they come to Him in repentance His arms are not wide open to accept and love them. Understanding this is critical to being healed from the consequences of all forms of rejection.

In God's created order, He intended every generation of children to learn about His character and nature, conveyed to them through the character and nature of their parents. But when man sinned the heart of man became distorted. As a result, the image of God that children receive from their parents is no longer a true reflection of His character and nature.

So, God sent His Son not only to be our Saviour from sin, but also to show us what the Father is really like. Because there was no sin in Jesus, His heart remained pure and when we look at Him we are looking at a true reflection of who God is, and we can, therefore, trust Him.

As we saw in Chapter 2, many people have received a false understanding of what God is like from the image that has been portrayed to them through their human parenting, especially their father. Because, in God's created order, children were intended to learn about Him from their parents, we need to ask ourselves what image of God did we get when we were growing up?

If it is a wrong image, then we need to forgive our parents for what they did, perhaps unknowingly. And we need to ask God to forgive us for believing a lie about who He really is, or what He is like. Then we need to ask Jesus to show us afresh what His Father is truly like. If we ask Him, He will then help us by His Holy Spirit to begin to accept and embrace God as He really is.

Just as I am – I come!

We are now beginning to grasp the fact that God really loves us. Jesus told the story of the prodigal son to teach us that no-one has strayed so far from the straight and narrow that they cannot return to God and come running into the Father's arms. With His help we can start to put a new foundation down for our lives.

In coming to God, we need to come just as we are! We may be able to clean up our outer skin with soap and water, but there is no such human remedy for cleaning up the inner self. We need a divine remedy! People can 'turn over a new leaf' meaning that they have put a line under the past and are trying to start again. But covering over the past in this way, just leaves the past unhealed and the heart unchanged.

If, in the past, there has been a moral, financial or even criminal failure, which has caused guilt and grief down the years and, just like David, this sin is ever before you (Psalm 51:3), there is nothing you can do to clean yourself up before coming to God. Frequently people try to do things for God, in an attempt to make up for what they have done wrong, things like giving money to charity or doing good works.

But no amount of giving or good works can atone for sin. All we can do – and this is everything we could possibly need – is follow the advice of the old hymn and say to God, *"Just as I am – I come!"* The Gospel invitation is an invitation to a "Come as you are party!" There is no other way!

Allowing God to accept us just as we are is a massive step toward the deepest level of healing we can ever experience. There are then no barriers to God's grace working a miracle in our hearts.

Knowing, accepting and loving myself

It's one thing to accept God as He is and to come to Him just as we are. But some people really struggle with the next step on our journey, accepting and loving themselves! They believe that God loves everyone else, but not them! They are embarrassed or ashamed about themselves and do all they can to cover up the reality of their own personhood. They have fallen out of love with who they are or, maybe, have never learned to love themselves in the first place.

They think that if they could improve themselves a bit, they would be more acceptable to God. But nothing could be farther from the truth! God already knows everything about us and still loves each one of us – every single member of His creation, irrespective of what may have happened along the way, to hurt them and damage their image.

Choosing to own this truth about ourselves is a huge step, which releases God to change us from the inside out so that we will become the person, restored in Him, that He made us to be. Believing that we are important to God and that our lives are significant and worthwhile means that we can then be free to really get to know and love who we are and enjoy the natural gifts God has given us. Ephesians 2: 10 tells us that God has prepared in advance things for us to do. And that means He has blessed us with the right natural gifts and abilities to do those things.

As we stop trying to be like someone else and learn to accept and love the person God has made us to be, the joy of the Lord becomes the strength of our inner being (Nehemiah 8:10). Sometimes people have squeezed themselves into an uncomfortable mould because of the expectations, desires or pressures of parents, siblings and teachers. Realising this uncomfortable fact provides an opportunity for forgiveness and a reassessment of life's opportunities and potential, including the possibility of new careers or new ways of serving the Lord or the development of new recreations or hobbies.

On many occasions I have seen that when a person starts to love themselves, hidden gifts and abilities come to the surface and it is as if they are released into a renewed season of life, which sometimes feels like a brand new life! Sometimes people say things like, *"I feel as though I've been born again – again!"* When they were born again they received new life in Christ, but now that life could develop to the fullness of its potential.

I remember one particular man who had always been striving to be the person his father wanted him to be – a doctor. His father had been unable to go to medical school because of the war, and as a result made a vow that if he ever had a son of his own, the boy would become the doctor that he'd never been able to be. When that son came along, he was a very practical boy with a technical mind and he really wanted to be an engineer. But, in order to please his father he went to medical school and became a doctor.

In mid-life, however, he was so depressed he had to take early retirement from the profession – he couldn't carry on. He'd been living a life which God had not gifted him for. As soon as he had forgiven his father and we prayed healing into his whole personality, his depression lifted and he was, at last, free to become the person that God had designed him to be.

Other people have felt undervalued and so they have tried to copy someone else whom they admired. But, in so doing, they were living a false life without joy or fulfilment. So, owning and being at peace with the person you are, thanking God for your gifts and abilities and then looking to Him to lead you into what is now best for you, can lead to very significant healing, wholeness and freedom.

Accepting others

Accepting others as they are is sometimes really hard, especially if we have to live or work with people who really get under our skin! But once we realise that God has accepted us as we are, and that we are to treat others in a similar way, God can change our heart attitude – even towards the most difficult of people. And I have noticed a divine law at work over the years – when we start accepting people as they are, they actually start to become more acceptable!

Accepting others does not mean we have to agree with their behaviour, or what they think or do. But it does mean by God's grace at work in us that we start relating with them differently. When we stop rejecting others and we start loving them unconditionally, God changes both our and their heart in the process.

This is also a great opportunity to think through all the episodes of life and remember the times we have been hurt by the rejection of others – especially by the things they have said and done which have left us angry and hurting on the inside. This is another opportunity to revisit our forgiveness list! And perhaps, also, we need to repent for those times when we have not accepted others in the past and hurt them through our own actions.

In conclusion

In the last chapter, we looked at four key aspects of forgiveness. And in this chapter we have discovered four key aspects of acceptance – accepting God as He is, allowing Him to accept us as we are, accepting ourselves and accepting others.

Forgiveness and acceptance are two foundational principles which are very closely tied together. It has been shown on thousands of occasions that if, by the power of the Holy Spirit, we can get these principles well-established in our lives, it transforms our inner being and strengthens us for living life in God's way.

Experiences of rejection, and our response to them, can become the territory of evil spirits, especially when the attitude of our own hearts is sinful. The demonic takes advantage of inner pain and offers false comfort on the inside, leading to people turning in on themselves and ceasing to live life to the full in the way that God intended. But living a life of forgiving others for all those times when we experience the pain of rejection and choosing not to treat others in a similar way, creates a healthy environment for spiritual growth and recovery of one's true identity – and removes any ground on which the enemy might want to stand.

We are beginning to understand that the process of discovering wholeness and freedom, is largely yielding to the work of the Holy Spirit in us and getting our lives into a right and godly order. As we shared earlier, the restoration of God's order in our lives is the foundational key to all discipleship and healing issues.

A Prayer to Help You

Thank You, Jesus, that You suffered the ultimate rejection on the cross, so that as a forgiven sinner I could be made totally acceptable to God. Thank You for showing us what Father God is really like in the story You told about the prodigal son.

I recognise that there is nothing I can do to make myself more acceptable or more lovable to You. I'm so grateful that You accept me just as I am and that You can then begin to work in my life to change me from the inside out so that I become more like you.

I thank You for the person that You made me to be. Help me to develop all the creative gifts and abilities that I have so that I will more fully be aware of Your plans and purposes for my life.

And help me, Lord, to accept others – even when I find them difficult, so that they will be touched by the love You give me in my heart for them.

In Jesus' Name, Amen.

CHAPTER 6

Setting the Captives Free

Discovering freedom from Satan's control

Introducing deliverance

Some people may be surprised to find a chapter on deliverance from demons in a book on healing! Perhaps the disciples were also surprised to find Jesus teaching them about deliverance as well. But remember that Jesus was without sin, which meant that, unlike any other human being, He had never come under Satan's control or authority. He was still, therefore, in a position of authority over Satan and, therefore, over all the powers of darkness under Satan's control. So, when HeeHe found people labouring under demonic bondage, He used His power and authority to set them free.

And when Jesus sent the disciples out to do the works of the Kingdom of God, He told them to use His power and authority and go and do the same things that He was doing (Luke 9:1-2) – including deliverance. The disciples did so and came back rejoicing at what they had seen God do as they obeyed Jesus

(Luke 10:17). And when the work of Ellel Ministries began in 1986, we were amazed to find how many of God's people on those early Healing Retreats were also in need of deliverance. It was thrilling to see how Jesus set them free and healed them.

Val had been chronically anorexic for fourteen years and was only able to take liquids. She was so distressed and without hope that she had told God she would commit suicide if He didn't do something. On our very first Healing Retreat she began to get her life in order in the ways we have already been sharing in the first five chapters. She made Jesus Lord of her life, she was filled with the Holy Spirit and then, in her case, God delivered her of the curse of death which was destroying her life. Thirty years later, after twenty years as a Salvation Army Pastor, she is now retired and a member of our ministry team at Ellel Grange! God worked a miracle of healing and deliverance in her life and she has never looked back.

So, let's get back to what the Bible says about this ministry of Jesus. When Isaiah prophesied about the coming of the Messiah in Isaiah 61 verses 1-4, he gave detailed attention to some of the things that the Sovereign Lord (Jesus) would do when He came. He said that Jesus would bind up the broken-hearted, proclaim freedom for the captives and release from darkness for prisoners.

Then, when Jesus began His ministry, as recorded in Luke 4:16-19, He expanded on this verse and said He would also set at liberty those who are oppressed. And it wasn't long after this that Jesus started to heal people by delivering them of evil spirits. The following Sabbath a man was delivered and healed in the synagogue at Capernaum and the people were amazed at His power and His authority as He set this man free.

Throughout His ministry Jesus healed people in different

ways, according to their condition and need. But setting people free from Satan's influence, through deliverance from evil spirits, was always an important part of both His and His disciples' ministry. In Luke 9:1-2 Jesus sent His own disciples out to proclaim the Kingdom of God and to heal the sick and to cast out demons. In the Acts of the Apostles deliverance was continued as part of the healing ministry of the embryonic church. And in Peter's sermon in Acts 10:38 he said that *"Jesus went around doing good and healing all those who were under the power of the devil because God was with him."*

Paul warned the Church at Ephesus about allowing ungodly behaviour among the people of God, telling them not to give a foothold to the devil (Ephesians 4:27). In Ephesians 6 Paul gave that remarkable teaching about how believers living the Christian life need to be wearing effective spiritual armour against Satan so that they *"will be able to stand against the schemes of the devil"* (Ephesians 6:11).

In 2 Corinthians 2:11 Paul says that he was not *"unaware of Satan's schemes"*. And in his first letter Peter warns believers that *"your enemy the devil prowls around like a roaring lion, looking for someone to devour. Resist him, standing firm in the faith"* (1 Peter 5:8-9). Finally, in the Lord's Prayer, Jesus taught His disciples to pray *"Deliver us from evil"* or, more accurately, *"Deliver us from the evil one"* (Matthew 6:19).

We cannot ignore these many references to the Kingdom work of deliverance from Satan's presence in people's lives. All the records of the early church fathers give accounts of how believers were delivered and healed from evil spirits. And there are reports throughout Christian history of people being delivered and healed – right up to the present time. When the work of Ellel Ministries first began, we were not looking to begin a deliverance ministry, but were simply responding to the vision God had given me, sixteen years previously, to minister healing and restoration to hurting and damaged people.

But for some of those in need of healing, deliverance very quickly became an essential tool to deal with the manifestations of the enemy, that were being brought into the light by God's anointing on the work. So much so, that I found it necessary to write *Healing Through Deliverance* (also available from Sovereign World). This book has been used to teach and train our own teams, and equip other ministries across the world who were coming up against the same difficulties, as they sought to minister God's healing. We soon realised that a healing ministry which does not embrace deliverance is putting serious limitations on what Jesus commissioned His followers to do.

How Satan can influence and control our lives

At the time of the Fall, as recorded in Genesis 3, Satan's primary tactic was to make man doubt what God had said. Once a person has started to question the authenticity and the authority of God, then they have gone most of the way towards rebellion and consequential disobedience (sin). Satan hasn't changed in his tactics and strategy. If we doubt the authority of God and His Word, we will cease to follow and obey Him.

Sin gives Satan rights. Humanity had been given, by God, authority over Planet Earth (dominionship or rulership, Genesis 1:28), but when human beings sinned by submitting themselves to Satan's authority, Satan won the right to take over mankind's earthly destiny and became the ruler of this world and has been influencing and impacting it ever since. He even tried to rob Jesus of His authority during His time of temptation in the wilderness (Luke 4:5-7).

Jesus described Satan as the ruler of this world (John 12:31 and 14:30). Paul described him as the god of this world (2 Corinthians 4:4) and John said that the whole world is under the control of the evil one (1 John 5:19). As such, everyone is influenced by who Satan is and by what he does through using the authority that human beings have given him. You cannot open any newspaper without seeing evidence of his presence and work in society around us and in the nations of the world.

Even when we are born again of the Spirit of God we still have to wrestle, as human beings, with the temptations of the enemy and with the reality of our own fallen nature, which has a natural desire to do what is wrong. Paul expressed it this way in Romans 7:19: I find it difficult to do the good things I want to do, and the bad things that I don't want to do come all too easily! Paul was simply echoing the reality of the human (carnal) nature that each one of us has.

When it comes to personal temptation, Satan first opens our eyes to the possibilities, then encourages us to think about them, as a pre-cursor to persuading us to follow through our thinking with actions. When we choose to sin, we are not only further damaging our relationship with God but, in Paul's words, inviting Satan to have a foothold in our lives (Ephesians 4:27).

When we realise that we have done wrong, we can come back to the cross in repentance and ask Jesus for forgiveness and healing. But if that doesn't happen, it's as if we are inviting Satan, or his agents, to oppress us. Then, sometimes, that oppression takes a step further and instead of experiencing oppression from the outside, the enemy moves inside and oppresses us from within.

When Satan has gained access to our lives we are 'spiritually sick' and then need healing through deliverance, otherwise the ongoing demonic presence on the inside can lead to all sorts of consequential symptoms, including physical conditions.

Jesus Came to set the captives free

Every human being is born into a fallen world – and that means, ultimately, that everyone is under the rulership of Satan, the god of this world, and under the same judgement of eternal separation from God (spiritual death) as Satan. But Jesus was without sin when He died and, therefore, not subject to Satan and the curse of death. So, when He died, death and Satan had no control over Him and when God raised Him from the dead He had overcome the curse of death for the whole of mankind.

The heart of the Gospel is that Jesus died to overcome sin and death and that all those who believe in Him and receive Him as Saviour are restored into a rightful relationship with the Father, as children of the living God (John 1:12). Salvation is, therefore, the ultimate deliverance for mankind from being under the curse of eternal death.

But, the deliverance of Jesus is not just from the curse of Satan's control in eternity, for He began his earthly ministry by declaring to everyone at the Nazareth synagogue that the work of healing and deliverance was about to begin here on Earth. He followed this up by ministering to people wherever He went and when deliverance was needed – whether it was the woman in Luke 13 with a bent back or the epileptic boy in Luke 9 – He addressed the enemy directly and set the captives free.

Today, Jesus is still setting the captives free through deliverance in fulfilment of the commission He gave to His first disciples. Then, through the great commission, Jesus commissioned the whole of the church, for the whole of time, to keep on doing the things that He taught those first disciples to do (Matthew 28:18-20).

Closing the Door to the Enemy

When Paul told believers (Ephesians 4:27) not to give Satan a foothold in their lives, he was giving them very practical advice. And in much of Ephesians chapters 4 and 5, he was reminding them of all the different ungodly things that they, as believing Christians, should avoid doing. He didn't want followers of Jesus to be ignorant of how the enemy wanted to invade their lives and throw them off course in their journey of faith.

And in his letter to the Galatians Paul said some very similar things – as did all the New Testament writers. It's clear that there is a direct relationship between the ongoing practice of sinful things and the increasing influence of a demonic presence in people's lives. And, today, nothing has changed!

In his letter to the Philippians, Paul made a list of the things that should be the focus of our lives, *"Whatsoever things are true, honest, just, pure, lovely, and of good report"* (Philippians 4:8). We should think on those things that can be described in this sort of way and not give over our mind to thinking ungodly thoughts. If our actions follow on from this kind of godly thinking, then there is no way that the enemy will gain any ground in our lives.

But, if we are willingly involved in things like wrong relationships, unclean thinking, watching pornography, dishonest words and actions, sinful anger, or out of control and unrighteous behaviour, then we need to be aware that we are living life in a danger zone and Satan, who is a legalist, will try and take advantage of every opportunity we give him.

It's good spiritual housekeeping in our daily devotions, to end each day with a personal review of our thoughts, words and actions of the day, so we can deal right away with anything that was sinful. And, also, we need to be careful to forgive any who have hurt us, remembering the principles we looked at in Chapter 4, so that no root of bitterness will grow up in our hearts. A root of bitterness is attractive ground for an evil spirit to prosper in.

If we live our lives for the Lord, and remove any ground on which the enemy could put his feet, then we will not be troubled by the enemy within. But if we give ground to his influence, then we shouldn't be surprised if, before long, we are not just wrestling with his influence, but with his presence.

Healing through deliverance

There are four primary ways through which unclean spirits can be given access into a person's life. *Firstly,* a spirit can come down the generation lines because of the sins of our forebears; *secondly* a spirit may gain access as a result of things that other people have done to them, such as severe rejection, abuse and cruelty. *Thirdly*, by putting the welcome mat down to the enemy through their own sinful actions. And *fourthly*, through trauma caused by accidents or being caught up in dreadful incidents such as terrorism or the effects of war.

The Generation Lines

In respect of the generation lines, people can, at first, think how unreasonable it is that unclean spirits could have the right to influence their lives, even before they were born! On the face of it, I agree with them. But the fact is, God has made us with the capacity to receive spiritual blessings down our generation line, and Satan simply uses that channel, designed by God to be a channel of blessing, for his own ungodly purposes (see Exodus 20:5).

On countless occasions, I have prayed for people who did not realise that they had been labouring all their lives under such generational demonic influence. But when they had forgiven all their ancestors for the consequences of their sins in the ancestral line, and prayed that Jesus would set them free, deliverance and healing has taken place.

For example, James had been a chronic epileptic since being a baby. He had a fit during a meeting and even though he was unconscious at the time, when I took him through a prayer of forgiveness of his ancestors, for whatever had been at the root of his epileptic condition, he was totally delivered and healed and never had another fit. The doctors who had been treating him for sixteen years were amazed!

When we first start on a journey of healing, therefore, it's good to begin by forgiving all those on our ancestral lines who have done things which may have given access to an evil spirit to curse one generation after another. This has been especially significant in the case of generational sexual sin, any form of occult activity or, sometimes, recurring physical conditions which are repeated in one generation after another.

Things That Have Happened to Us

Then, with regard to the second potential issue, we may also need to do quite a lot of forgiving of those who have hurt us in our own lifetime. Things that have caused us pain, and which we have tried to get over by pushing them down and moving on with life. But when we push things down like that, we push them down unhealed. And unhealed pain can fester and cause us personal problems.

Our Own Sins

Thirdly, there may be a lot of things in our own past which we hadn't previously dealt with before the Lord – things from before we became a Christian and afterwards as well. So, initially, there may be quite a lot of things to confess and pray through with a humble heart, as we continue to discover more of the healing that God has for us, and for some of these things we may also need cleansing through deliverance.

There can be wrong relationships that have resulted in ungodly soul ties (see more about this in Chapter 7) and the enemy can be using those to gain access to our lives. And, commonly, people have, from time to time, dabbled in things of the occult and deliberately opened a doorway into the wrong supernatural realms, and so invited ungodly spiritual power into their lives.

Accidents and Traumas

Lastly, we have found that many people have needed deep healing from the consequences of accidents or traumas they have experienced during their lifetime (see more about this in Chapter 8). When people have been traumatised in this way, the trauma can have the effect of holding open a doorway of fear, through which evil spirits can enter and then hold people into their bondage. On many, many occasions we have seen people set free and healed, of even long-term consequences, conditions and injuries, as God has healed them through deliverance and emotional healing. God loves us and knows what is best for us – so we can trust Him.

In conclusion

From the very first *Healing Retreat* at Ellel Grange to the present day, we have seen people's lives constantly being transformed through deliverance as part of the healing prayer ministry they have received. Jesus came to set the captives free and it is important that the Body of Christ faithfully ministers to people in the ways that Jesus first taught His disciples – and that always included deliverance where necessary. God has been restoring the healing and deliverance ministries to His church, and it is thrilling to see His people enter into their freedom as those who were prisoners are released from the darkness of the enemy's hold on their lives.

Deliverance is not something to be afraid of. If we care-fully deal with all the reasons why a spirit may have gained access to people's lives and exercised authority in them, then we can simply address any spirit and order it, in Jesus' name to leave. Sometimes there may be some physical evidence of the spirit leaving such as coughing or heavy breathing, but not always. Some of the most profound healings through deliverance have taken place without anything immediately obvious happening – but the person knows inside that something has changed – freedom and wholeness has come to 'their house'!

A Prayer to Help You

Thank You, Lord, that You taught us to pray 'Deliver us from the evil one' in 'the Lord's prayer'. And thank You for demonstrating how when You delivered people of evil spirits that they got healed.

I recognise that when mankind sinned Satan became god of this world and that as a believer I need to be on my guard against temptations and attacks from the evil one. I am sorry for those times in my life when through my own sin I have laid down a welcome mat to the enemy. Help me to deal with every spirit that has gained entrance to my life in this way that I might be set free.

And where Satan has gained entry through my generational line or what others have done to me, I forgive all those who have hurt me and ask You, Jesus, to set me free from the influence or control of every evil spirit that took advantage of those situations.

I pray, Lord, that You will set me free from every evil presence and influence in my life. In Jesus' Name, Amen

CHAPTER 7

Healing for My Relational Past

Discovering healing from wrong relationships

God is a relational God – He is Father, Son and Holy Spirit and they relate with each other in the absolute unity and one-ness of the Godhead. And we were made to have and enjoy relationship with Him as well as enjoy rightful relationships with other human beings.

Each and every one of us was knit together (Psalm 139:13) in the womb of a woman following a sexual relationship between a man and a woman or, very occasionally in these days, through implantation in the womb of an already fertilised egg, following *in vitro* fertilisation. It was God's original plan that this relationship would be between a woman and her husband within the confines of godly marriage. In the womb every baby has a totally dependent relationship with their mother.

And God's original intent was, also, that the mother should be under the spiritual and physical covering and protection of the man, who is the father of the child who has been conceived. This is God's ideal for marriage. It is also His ideal that, as children grow and mature into their own adulthood, their sexual relationships should be reserved for their marital partner alone.

But we all know that the reality of our fallen and sinful world has meant that many people have indulged in sexual relationship with other partners, and that the vast majority of people today come to their wedding ceremony (if they get married) having already anticipated their wedding night on many occasions.

Additionally, many children are conceived in less than ideal circumstances and, as already referred to in Chapter 1, in our amoral society as many as 25% of today's children are being brought up in one parent families, outside the protection of a covenantal marriage relationship. And a significant number, also, are being brought up by two parents in amalgamated families, with children of different mothers or fathers all being brought up together. The consequential physical, emotional and spiritual confusion and deprivation can be huge.

While most single parents do all they can to provide for their children, they can never fully compensate for the absence of either a father or a mother. This leaves huge holes in a child's personal well-being and robs them of much parental input and stability throughout their growing years.

When ministering to people later in life, the consequence of their relational past is often a significant factor in their current situation. But whatever the background has been, when we bring everything into the light, God is able to heal the hurt and pain arising from a difficult upbringing, as well as forgive the sin and heal the wounding sustained through relationships that were not as God intended.

We have seen many people's lives totally transformed as a result of them meeting the Healer at the deepest point of their relational need. God doesn't reject us because of either our sin or our hurts, but He does want things to be in the light, so they can be forgiven and healed.

Understanding God's created order for relationships

In establishing God's order for relationships, we can see that all three persons of the Trinity were involved in both creating our world as part of the universe and in the creation of mankind to live on Planet Earth. John Chapter 1 describes Jesus as the Word and says that *"the Word became flesh and dwelt among us"* (John 1:14). In verse 3 it says that *"without Him was not anything made that was made"*.

Genesis 1:2 describes the Holy Spirit's involvement in the work of creation and Genesis 1:26 refers to God as *"us"* in the decision to *"make man in our image and likeness."* It's clear from these and other Scriptures that God Himself is a relational trinity of Father, Son and Holy Spirit. And when God made human beings in His own image and likeness, He created mankind to also be a relational trinity – a trinity of body, soul and spirit, with all three being in relational harmony and unity with each other, as we saw right at the beginning of our journey of discovery.

Mankind was also created as a race of sexually different men and women who would be attracted to each other. Through sexual relationships they would be able to reproduce themselves, so that the children born to mankind would also be made in the image and likeness of God.

God's intention was that men and women should be joined together as *"one flesh"* through sexual intercourse and provide a secure means of God's covering for their children, as parents. The joining together of man and woman is not just a physical act, for the whole of man and the whole of woman, spirit, soul and body, is involved. Following the physical joining of sexual intercourse, the spirit and the soul remain connected. Something of the personhood of the man is received by the woman and something of the personhood of the woman is received by the man. This was God's intention for marriage.

It is through this sexual act that a marriage is consum-mated, which means 'bring the marriage to completion'. The church has always taught that if a marriage has not been consummated then the marriage relationship and vows can be annulled – for that which is necessary to complete a marriage has not taken place. It is not, therefore, a marriage. It is only when consummation has taken place that the relationship can overflow into a full spiritual union, when a couple truly become one with and part of each other.

Marriage is used in the Scripture to be a picture of the relationship between Jesus, the Bridegroom, and mankind, the Bride. A believer is described many times as being "in Christ", but the relationship between Jesus and mankind is also described as Christ being in us. And that is exactly how God intended a marital relationship to be, with the husband and the wife being in and part of each other.

It is this total union that leads to husband and wife being able to grow like each other as the years go by, sometimes even, to the extent that, with time, physical similarities can develop. In just the same way as human beings take on the characteristics of godliness the longer they have known the Lord (2 Corinthians 3:18), husband and wife grow together in their likeness to each other.

It is the security of God's intended marital relationship for man and woman, with love for each other at its heart, that provides the generational security for children to grow up in. Their experience of the knowledge and love of God through their parenting, equips them for their own adulthood and coming to know God for themselves. They are then able to pass on to one generation after another the privilege of living in a covenant relationship with God and with each other.

God is a God of covenant love for His creation. And marriage is also a covenant, reflecting in the relationship between husband and wife, the relationship God desires to have with His people. We were made to have and enjoy relationship with Him and have and enjoy rightful relationships with other human beings.

The consequences of sexual sin

At the time of the Fall, as recorded in Genesis 1-3, Satan's primary tactic was to throw doubt on what God had said. Once a person has started to question the authority of God, they have started on a journey towards rebellion and consequential disobedience (sin). Satan hasn't changed in his tactics and strategy. If we doubt the authority of God and His Word, we will cease to follow and obey Him.

The past two hundred years has seen a progressive turning away from and doubting of God and His word in the majority of the world. In the UK, teaching that God is Creator has been dismissed from our schools. A meaningful act of daily worship in our schools is largely a thing of the past. And public respect for God's Word, His commandments and the truth of Jesus has all but disappeared from the market-place of life. Instead of being respected for their faith and their stand, those who choose to live according to their belief in Jesus, have more often than not become the object of ridicule.

And nowhere more so is this the case than in the whole arena of sexual behaviour and relationships. Instead of children being prepared in their upbringing for godly marriage they are, instead, prepared for promiscuity by sex education without morality and by making contraceptives freely available to them. Today's children are practising openly what previous generations were sometimes guilty of privately. The wind of change has become a whirlwind of license.

So why does all this matter? Why is it so clear, throughout God's Word, that sexual sin, by which we primarily mean in this section, fornication and adultery, is consistently forbidden. The answer lies back there in our understanding of Godly marriage. We learned that when two people enter into a sexual relationship it is not just their bodies that are being joined in the thrill of a sexual moment, but because God created mankind with spirit, soul and body, all three components of our creation are involved. And after the act of physical union is over the two people remain joined together through their spirit and their soul, irrespective of whether or not they are married. The union has been consummated.

This is what God has ordained for sexual relationships and God cannot change His ordinances to allow men and women to enjoy so called 'free sex', without there being any subsequent joining or ongoing consequence. Every time a man and a woman have sex with each other something of each is given to the other and after sex is over, the emotional and spiritual union remains (1 Corinthians 6:16).

In marriage that is a good life-time bonding, but outside of marriage it becomes a life-lasting bondage in which something of that other person's spirit and soul has become part of you and you have given something of your own spirit and soul away to another person (Proverbs 5:15-22) – a soul-tie has been established with the other person. This can be a godly soul-tie if it's established within marriage, or an ungodly soul-tie if it's outside of marriage.

By entering into ungodly sexual relationships pre-marriage, people diminish their own God-given personality and take on board aspects of the personhood of those they have slept with. Which means that when people who have indulged in a promiscuous past come to make their marriage vows, they have already consummated relationships with other people. The person who is making those vows is, in fact, both more and less than God intended – the more, being the presence and influence of those other partners and the less, being that of themselves which they have given away to others.

All sexual sin is part of Satan's strategy to lead mankind ever deeper into rebellion against God. When we live our lives in obedience to God, He blesses us with His Holy Spirit. Conversely when we follow the pathways of Satan we are vulnerable to receiving not Holy Spirit, but an unclean spirit.

For this reason, when people come to the point of repenting over their sexual sin, they may also need deliverance from any spirit that was given access at the time the relationship took place. This can be a spirit of lust or, sometimes, spirits associated with any other unclean or occultic activities their sexual partners might have been involved in.

For those who get caught up in an act of adultery when already married, the situation is similar. The adulterer is joining themselves to someone else, who then becomes a third party, spiritually, in the marriage. One lady told me how her husband had just confessed to having committed adultery ten years previously. But she said, *"When my husband came back from that business weekend, I felt there was now someone else in the bed with us. I couldn't understand it at the time, but now I know I was right."*

The fact is, when people have multiple sexual relations, they take into their next relationship everyone they've previously been in relationship with. This vital principle became the subject of a national poster campaign in South Africa, in an attempt to limit the spread of sexually transmitted diseases. I photographed one advertisement which pictured a woman lying in a man's arms, but with these words across the top: *"Everyone he's slept with is sleeping with you."* The poster conveyed a message that went beyond the spread of a virus to the spread of spiritual bondage.

All of this sounds like bad news, but the good news is that God is able to undo those ungodly relationships (soul-ties), deliver us from the influence and presence of the enemy and restore us in His image and likeness. It is only He, who ordained what happens when men and women join themselves together sexually, who is able to undo the consequences of those relationships and release us afresh into our own unadulterated identity.

One man, who had worked in many countries, was deeply repentant of all the relationships he had had on his travels. He asked God to forgive and cleanse Him and in prayer I asked Jesus to break the ungodly soul-ties and restore him to being himself. Afterwards he described how he sensed all the components of his life which came from previous sexual partners leaving one after another. He could 'see' them returning to the people he had slept with. But he also saw everything of himself, that had been given away to others, being restored to his own being. At the end he said these remarkable words, *"I now feel as though I know who I am!"* Prior to that moment his whole being had been infiltrated by the presence and characteristics of his sexual partners.

Being honest with myself

The road to healing requires our own participation in the process. God longs to see us restored, but He cannot change our history. What has happened, has happened! But if we deal with our pride, come to Him in real repentance, asking Him for forgiveness, He will heal and restore us.

When David committed adultery, he was in denial of his own behaviour and continued to go into even deeper sin of denial, cover up and, eventually, murder. It was only when Nathan the prophet confronted him in his behaviour (2 Samuel 12) that he came under the conviction of the Holy Spirit and began his journey of faith and healing.

Nothing could change the facts of what David had done, but if you read Psalm 51 you will read about his personal spiritual journey after the event. In verse 6 he says to the Lord, *"Surely you require truth in the inner parts, you teach me wisdom in the inmost place"*. David realised that it was only when the wrong things that he had hidden in his heart had been brought to the light that it was possible for God to bring healing and restoration. His prayer in verse 16 sums up the cry of all those who are facing the facts of their own sexual sin, *"Create in me a pure heart, O God, and renew a steadfast spirit within me."*

David was desperately in need of God's healing and restoration. He feared most the removal of the Holy Spirit who had been with him since that very first day of his anointing by Samuel to be king (1 Samuel 16:13). David knew that unless God healed him, his spiritual life, which was so precious to him, was in grave danger. He was desperate for the joy of salvation to be restored to him. And God did hear and did answer the cry of his heart.

On countless occasions now, we have had to confront

some-one with the reality of unresolved guilt because of unconfessed sexual sin. On one occasion, I was praying for the healing of a lady's neck, which had been injured in an accident, sixteen years previously. But it was as if the Holy Spirit had been withdrawn and there seemed no anointing on my prayers. Then the Lord prompted me to ask her where she was going on that night when the accident occurred. She was deeply embarrassed to confess, *"I was on my way to commit adultery."* It was only when her sexual sin had come to the light and she had dealt with it before God, that I was free to pray for her again and this time God's healing love and presence overwhelmed her.

Our natural instinct is to cover up the things we have done wrong. That is because we all have a carnal nature as a result of the Fall, and pride says that we don't want other people to know about the things we're ashamed of. It's interesting that in James 5:16 we read how important it is to be sure that there is no unconfessed sin standing in the way of our healing when we ask for prayer.

Being honest with oneself is the first step towards being honest with the Lord. We all need to know that there is nothing so awful in our lives that God isn't willing to forgive, cleanse and heal. Some of the most powerful times of healing we have experienced in Ellel Ministries, have been when we have taught on the consequences of sexual sin and people have been convicted by the Holy Spirit and then, in humility, asked for prayer.

Satan would want us to keep the lid on those things that need to be brought to the light – for he knows that when they have been dealt with he will lose power to control people's lives. But God would want us to bring those hidden things into the light so that they may be dealt with once and for all and we can know His restoration, healing and deliverance.

Restored in the image of God

God's love for us is unconditional, for He IS love. Jesus died so that all our sins can be forgiven – without exception. So, we need not fear that by bringing things into the light we will somehow or other lose our relationship with the Lord. The reverse is the case. For if there are ungodly soul-ties which are still in place then the influence of those past relationships needs to be dealt with once and for all.

By asking God to forgive us for the sin and then break the ungodly soul-tie that has joined us to that person, we can then be set free through deliverance from any consequential demonic influence or presence. We simply command the demons to leave in the Name of Jesus. We can then ask God to restore whatever of ourselves we gave away through the relationship and ask Him to take away from us every influence from that sexual partner which has been making us live in ways that are contrary to His intentions.

When God forgives, delivers, heals and restores in this way, the potential for healing is huge. It is a life-transforming experience to rediscover one's own identity and then grow afresh as the person God intended us to be, restored again into His image and likeness, unimpeded by the controlling influence of ungodly soul ties.

God not only wants to restore us in this way, but He is then able to restore to us our destiny. For we are then freed from the ungodly influences of past relationships. We can then be freshly sensitive to the leading of His Spirit and hearing His voice as He takes us by the hand and leads us into His purposes for the rest of our lives. That is our prayer for each and every one that we are privileged to pray for.

Jesus knows us through and through. He knows all about the good and the bad and His love for us is unconditional. But if there have been ungodly sexual relationships in the past, then God doesn't want us to remain under the influence of previous sexual partners or any resulting demonic presence. He wants us to be free to serve Him and to know once again the joy of our salvation and His healing.

A Prayer to Help You

Thank You Lord, for instituting the covenant of marriage – Your best plan for human family relations hips and for the bringing up of children. I recognise that all sexual relationships outside the covenant of marriage are sinful and I ask You to forgive me for all ungodly relationships that I have had.

Where ungodly soul-ties have been established in my life I ask You to break them and restore to me everything of myself that I have wrongfully given away to others and to take away from me everything of other people that I have received into my life.

I take authority over every unclean spirit that has been given access to my life as a result of these relationships and order them to leave me now in the name of Jesus.

I choose now to bring all my relationships into Godly order. Cleanse me, I pray, and create in me a pure heart O God. In Jesus's Name, Amen

CHAPTER 8

Broken Through Wounding and Pain

Discovering healing from the traumas of the past

We saw at the beginning of our journey of discovery that, as human beings, we have three primary components to our nature – spirit, soul and body. Each one of them is capable of experiencing wounding and, therefore, pain.

There is the pain which God feels – spiritual pain. The sort of pain, for example, that our wilful involvement in rebellion and sinful behaviour must cause to a God who loves each one of us so much. Parents could feel just that sort of pain in their spirits also, if, and when, their own children choose to go into rebellion and adopt a lifestyle or make choices which are a long way from God's best.

Remember that our soul contains the mind with which we think and process information, the emotions with which we feel and react and the will with which we make decisions. Mental anguish and unresolved pain is at the root of many diagnosed psychological or psychiatric conditions. And then there is the pain in our emotions when we are hurt, for example, by the words or the actions of others. Physical tears are the body's way of helping the soul to express inner pain, which can also give God an opening to bring comfort to the wounding.

When inner pain is long-lasting, or severe, it can then begin to be felt physically in ways other than with tears. Many of the pain symptoms that bring people to their doctor for diagnosis and treatment are not, initially, caused by physical symptoms at all. But they can be the body's way of telling you that something's wrong on the inside.

One lady I prayed for was about to have an operation to investigate undiagnosed pain in her back. But during the time of prayer the Lord reminded her that her relationship with her husband's mother was causing great friction at home. She felt as though she was being stabbed in the back by things her mother-in-law said and did. When this emotional and spiritual wound had been faced, forgiveness offered, and the situation dealt with, the pain in the back was healed and she didn't need the operation!

Finally, there is straightforward physical, bodily pain caused by accidents, injuries or, sometimes, as a side effect of physical disease or bodily illness.

Diagnosing the root of pain can be a bit like diagnosing the reasons a car engine is not running very well. If you don't discover what the problem is by checking the various systems and put any malfunction right, much more damage could be done. Then, when you know what's causing the problem you can carry out a repair and restore the engine to its normal running condition. In a similar way it can be important to understand where the root of human pain is located, so we can pray specifically about the real problem.

One of the main reasons people are not healed when being

prayed for, is because we are praying for the wrong thing. We can be praying for healing of the symptoms, but not be dealing with the real issue.

One of the primary sources of unresolved pain – either pain affecting us on the inside in our spirit and soul or in the body, is trauma. We have discovered over many years that when God heals the person of the traumas, even though those traumas may have happened a long time ago, then He also heals them of consequential painful issues that they can have been experiencing right up to that day.

How trauma locks us into past experiences

A trauma is a sudden, unexpected event in life which causes extreme pain and distress. Traumas can be as varied as falling down stairs, being involved in a car accident, being sexually abused, receiving sudden bad news, painful medical investigations or, as was Lynda's experience, falling off a cliff on a night hike with her youth group and breaking her back in four places.

When you stretch an elastic band, it returns to its original length and shape when you remove the tension. But if you overstretch the elastic it suddenly snaps and cannot return to its original length and shape. At the point of snapping the elastic limit of the rubber band has been reached. Our inner being is a bit like a piece of human elastic! And suffering a trauma has the effect of stretching our inner being as we try to cope with whatever has happened.

God designed us to cope with all sorts of different experiences and our inner 'elastic' copes with most of life's events. But sometimes we experience something which pushes us beyond our elastic limit. And the younger we are when such extreme and stressful things happen, the more easily are we pushed beyond the elastic limit of our tolerance, and something snaps inside. When that happens something of the pain of the event gets locked away on the inside and when we choose to move on in life, we can then, subconsciously, leave behind that part of us which is carrying the pain.

Most minor traumas in adult life, which do not push us beyond our 'elastic limit' do not have long-lasting consequences, and we recover from them quite quickly. But when the trauma is serious, or the person is very young, we don't know how to handle the consequential pain, so we can then try to move on through life as if nothing has happened, leaving the painful experience behind. But when wounding and pain is locked away like that, it remains unhealed, still tied to the trauma of the event, and often causing symptoms which have a limiting effect on our capacity to enjoy life.

When Lynda fell off the cliff her body was badly broken and she experienced a trauma that pushed her beyond her ability to handle the pain. The doctors did their best to help her, but several years later she was still suffering inner pain which was trapped in that traumatised and broken part of her inner being. When we prayed for her we asked Jesus to bring that broken inner part out from her inner being so that He could heal the wound, take away the pain and restore her to wholeness. The full story of Lynda's miraculous healing is told in her own book, *"Lynda"* published by Sovereign World.

Jim was seriously betrayed by his father when only six years of age. Encouraged to jump into his Dad's arms from the top of a pile of hay bales, Jim jumped, but his Dad stood aside and let Jim crash onto the concrete below. That was more than six-year-old Jim could stand and he snapped inside. His chest was crushed on impact with the concrete and he shortly became asthmatic. When I first met Jim at age 51, he had been a chronic asthmatic for as long as he could remember.

But when we prayed for Jim, God brought that broken-hearted part of Jim to the surface of Jim's consciousness and the adult man, who had been standing there in front of us before, was now lying on the floor sobbing like a little boy. Jim had to forgive his Dad for doing such a terrible thing and God brought healing to that inner, broken and crushed little boy. But then we saw the miracle.

The physical symptoms of asthma, which had been like a living curse for the whole of his life, were wonderfully healed. The root of the asthma symptoms lay in his broken heart. The doctors had been treating his physical symptoms in the best way they knew how. But the real problem was the trauma that was locked on the inside. When that was healed, he no longer needed his medication!

Jesus came to heal the broken-hearted

When we first began to understand how trauma can affect our inner beings so profoundly and saw how people were being healed, we urgently needed to find this principle in the Scriptures. It wasn't long before we realised that healing of inner brokenness was right there in the prophetic passage in Isaiah 61:1 which describes what the Sovereign Lord, (the Messiah, Jesus) would do when He came.

Here, we read how He would *heal the broken-hearted and set the captives free.* And the Hebrew word that is used to express being broken, in the word broken-hearted, simply means *"shattered into separate pieces"*. Just like the tablets of stone, on which were written the ten commandments, when Moses threw them down to the ground (Exodus 32:19). You might say that the stone tablets were so traumatised that they had been stretched beyond their elastic limit!

It is this depth of healing that Isaiah was referring to when he said Jesus would heal the broken-hearted, for many people carry the consequences and scars of past traumas. In Luke 13:10-17 we read of Jesus healing a woman whose spine was bent double. He said that she had been bound by a spirit for eighteen years. We are not told what happened to her eighteen years ago, but it was clear that her physical body was desperately in need of healing as a result and she was suffering long term consequences of whatever it was that had happened eighteen years previously. When Jesus healed her, He was fulfilling the prophecy of Isaiah 61 – healing her broken heart and setting her free!

We have now seen hundreds of traumatised people, all over the world, being healed by Jesus. We have no hesitation, therefore, in saying that Jesus longs to heal not just the pain that people are suffering, but the inner reason for the pain, which caused the presenting problem in the first place.

The face of a woman in Ukraine had been distorted by rough forceps treatment at her birth. She and her husband were listening to this teaching on *Healing from Accident and Trauma* in an Ellel Ministries Conference and simultaneously applying the teaching to themselves. Suddenly the woman began to cry like a hurting baby as the Lord began to release pain from the inner part which had been trapped inside all those years.

But the greater miracle was the physical healing that she then received in her face, as the facial damage was healed and her adult face was restored as God intended her to be!

Letting God in to my broken past

It's often a huge surprise for people to realise that their present physical problems, inner distress or pain can be tied to inner brokenness that was locked away on the inside, many years ago. The first step towards healing, and sometimes deliverance also, is to recognise that there might be a link between today's problem and yesterday's traumatic event.

Many people don't like to face the reality of their past – they have moved on in life and want to just live life as it is! But sometimes there are long-hidden issues which are preventing them from doing so – and they then begin to look for answers. Letting God into our past can prove to be a vital step towards healing.

Giving God permission to show us those things that have happened to us in the past, which are still affecting us today, opens the door for the Holy Spirit to expose sources of pain and problems, and start the work of healing. Sometimes those issues can involve difficult relationships and as we have already seen in earlier chapters, people would prefer not to think about the effect of these on their lives – especially if that step is going to involve forgiving people for what they have done.

One lady, in her forties, was still struggling with severe neck pain arising from a motor-bike accident many years earlier. The driver lost control and she, the pillion passenger, was thrown into the air and landed on her head. When facing up to the need to forgive, she very bitterly said, *"Forgive him, why should I, he's ruined my life."*

Her statement was true – he had ruined her life – but continuing to hold him in unforgiveness was ruining her life even more. She had been severely traumatised emotionally and physically, by the accident. The inner brokenness was serious, but it was only when she faced up to the need to forgive that God was able to reach down into her broken past. He healed her broken-heartedness and then the physical problems got healed also! The following day she found she was able to do things physically that she had not been able to do since before the accident.

Saying *'Yes'* to God and giving Him permission to expose anything from our past, however, painful it is, that might hold a key to inner brokenness can be a vital step on our journey of healing.

Healing from the consequences of accidents

On a 9-week Flagship School at Ellel Grange, an Indian woman struggled with sitting for long periods of time during the teaching sessions. Her spine was in considerable pain and it was difficult for her to stay in the sessions. In the third week, she listened to the teaching about trauma and inner brokenness and remembered an occasion at primary school when someone pulled her chair away just as she was about to sit down. She fell very painfully onto her lower spine. It was a very simple thing for her to forgive the person who had deliberately caused the accident, and to ask Jesus to heal the inner brokenness caused by a trauma which, at her then tender age, had taken her beyond her 'elastic limit'. The healing of the back was immediate, and she enjoyed the rest of the school without any problem in sitting through the teaching sessions!

In healing conferences or training schools, I often ask people to think back through their lives and write down on a piece of paper brief details of any accident or trauma they have suffered and whether or not they are still struggling to cope with any consequential symptoms. We will never cease to be surprised at the range of accidents that people have suffered and the extent of current physical disorder and pain that some people still have as a result. Our teams then pray with as many people as possible.

The process of praying is very straightforward. We ask who caused the accident and is there a forgiveness issue still associated with the incident. Most people have never even thought that there was a need to forgive and are genuinely surprised by the question. When they realise the importance of forgiving, most people have no problem in following Jesus' guidelines in the Lord's prayer in Matthew 6, which can be summarised as *forgive us for the things we've done wrong as we forgive others for what they have done to us.*

Sometimes, we face situations where the accident was the person's own fault – and, in those cases, we ask people to seek God's forgiveness for their carelessness and, even, forgive themselves! For many people have come through such accidents, saying such things as *"I'll never forgive myself for what happened."* In reality, when they say such thing, as we learned back in Chapter 4, it's as if they are cursing themselves. It's not surprising, therefore, that there are long-term unhealed symptoms.

We then ask the Lord to expose any traumatised and broken part of their being and ask Him to heal the broken heart, as is promised in the Scriptures (Isaiah 61:1). We then ask the Lord to set the captive free, through deliverance of any unclean spirit, which took advantage of the trauma. It has been such a privilege to pray with and see so many people made whole by the living God, as the Holy Spirit works a miracle of healing in their lives.

One lady in her sixties had suffered most of her life with acute, undiagnosed, left-chest pain. Her doctors had not been able to identify the root of the problem and she was on the verge of having investigative surgery. When we prayed with her, we asked the Lord to bring to her memory anything that could have caused the problem in the first place. As we prayed she remembered that as a very young child she was severely ill and had fluid on her left lung. Where they were living at the time, there were no such things as anaesthetics available to numb the pain and in order to save her life, a nurse had to pierce the lung, through the chest wall, with a wide needle and suck out the fluid. The pain had been excruciating. Sixty years later we asked the Lord to heal her traumatised and broken heart, as she forgave the medics for causing so much pain while doing what they had to do. The Lord graciously drew the pain out of her chest, she was delivered of a spirit of infirmity and she was totally and quickly healed.

In conclusion

As God gave us understanding of what can happen when people are traumatised through sudden events such as accidents, we learned to ask people, who were suffering long-term problems, if they had had any accidents or traumas in their lives. The keys God has given often opened the door to a life-changing encounter with the living God, bringing hope, healing and restoration.

In many cases, what God did to bring such healing became a

powerful witness to His supernatural power, resulting in others being drawn to the Lord. No wonder Jesus sent the disciples out to both preach the Kingdom of God and to heal the sick! To read further on this subject please refer to my book *"Healing from the Consequences of Accident, Shock and Trauma,"* also published by Sovereign World.

A Prayer to Help You

Thank You, Jesus, that You came to heal the hearts of those who have been broken on the inside through the traumas of life. Help me to remember those events in my life which were too painful for me to bear at the time and through which I may have been broken on the inside.

I forgive anyone and everyone who was involved in the events that caused me such pain, including myself. I pray that You will touch every part of me that has been broken, heal and restore it so that all the fractures in my soul and spirit may be completely healed.

I pray then that where my body has been unhealed because of the brokenness on the inside that You will now heal me physically so that I will no longer have to carry any of the pain associated with those things that happened to me in the past. Thank You for paying the price for my healing. In Jesus' Name, Amen.

CHAPTER 9

Freedom from Fear

Discovering freedom from fears that control

None of us like to admit that we have a problem with fear, especially when the fear can seem so irrational to others. But the fact is that, for many people, fear has become a serious, even a controlling issue, in their lives. Fear can have the effect of limiting both our activities and our enjoyment of life. The list of possible fears that people can have is endless, but here's a few for starters!

Fear of dogs
Fear of flying
Fear of spiders
Fear of snakes
Fear of wasps
Fear of open spaces
Fear of being shut in
Fear of dying
Fear of rejection
Fear of failure

A fear which has such a grip on someone that it is controlling their behaviour, is generally known as a phobia. For example, the fear of spiders is known as *arachnophobia* and the fear of being shut in is *claustrophobia*.

There is a natural thought process and emotional response to some circumstances which would make us want to avoid things that could hurt or harm us. For example, most of us would treat the sudden appearance of a snake, with a degree of alarm. For some people, however, their natural caution over such things has gone beyond being a sensible reaction and has become something totally irrational and controlling.

Often there is some event in life which is at the root of such irrational fears. My mother had a cousin who was terrified of going near a circus. For her this was totally reasonable, having been bitten by an escaped tiger on her first and last visit to the big top! No amount of careful explanation of improved safety precautions could persuade her to overcome the gripping fear that was now on the inside. The reason for this is usually because a demonic spirit of fear has gained access through the trauma.

It is a fact that during moments of great fear or trauma, people are spiritually vulnerable. A road accident, for example, is a physically dramatic, even tragic, event. But it can also be a prime opportunity for demons to take advantage of the traumatized state that accident victims are often in. It is only much later, often years later, when the person is still suffering the effects of the accident, that we have been able to piece together what actually happened as healing and deliverance has taken place.

At one conference, a lady explained that she had taken quarter of an hour longer to get there than it should have done – for the simple reason that she always avoided driving on the road which would have brought her by the quickest route. Many years earlier she had been driving on that road and became tangled up in the consequences of a car accident that had happened in front of her.

As a result, she had a great fear of being terribly injured, or even dying, if she travelled on that road, and the fear became such a controlling influence that she would drive several miles out of her way to avoid going on the stretch of road where the accident had happened. She was controlled by the fear. During the conference, she was set free from the spirit of fear that had come into her and the following day she was rejoicing at having driven on the quick route without any fear. Jesus had set her free and healed her through deliverance.

In dealing with many such cases across the years, we have seen how a spirit entered and made the person afraid of driving, or travelling, on a particular stretch of road. In all cases the effect was long-lasting and had been made much worse by the controlling influence of spirits of fear. But that means it was curable through deliverance, provided that the person was willing to forgive anyone responsible (including themselves where necessary) and make a choice not to let the fear control their lives, but rather trust Jesus.

Many times, Jesus said things like "Do not fear". If we choose to be afraid then we are opening the door to being controlled by a spirit of fear. And the message from Scripture, that Jesus came to set the captives free, is outstandingly good news for those whose lives are controlled by fear.

Good and bad fears!

While fear is one of the most powerful factors that can control the conduct of many people's lives, it may surprise you to know that there is also a beneficial fear, that will keep us from doing harmful things. There are two kinds of fear that are gifts of God.

Firstly, there is holy fear of a Holy God. In Exodus 20:20, Moses told the people that it is the fear of the Lord that will keep them from sinning. And anything that keeps us from giving in to the rebellion of sin must be a good thing. Such holy fear is an outworking of love for and worship of the Holy God, the Creator of all things, who weighs all the affairs of mankind and the lives of individual men and women (Proverbs 21:2).

You may remember those amazing words to Belshazzar which were supernaturally written on the wall of his palace during a banquet, and which Daniel interpreted for him: *"You are weighed in the balance and found wanting"* (Daniel 5:27). Because he had no fear of the living God, his life had been lived according to his own self-centred wishes and God's judgement was upon him.

And then, in Hebrews 11:7, we read how fear of God kept Noah on the right track in building the ark for the salvation of mankind. It says that, *"in holy fear he built the ark."* Without such holy fear, Noah would never have had the tenacity and endurance to complete the building of the ark over such a long period of time, especially when there had been no sign of the sort of rain which would bring about a flood. Holy fear and godly obedience are companions which help us to fulfil the purposes of God in our lives.

Secondly, without the other kind of godly fear, very few people would survive childhood, such are the risks and dangers that we all face day by day. We learn to be afraid, for example, of such things as putting our hand in the fire, of falling from a great height or crossing the road in the midst of traffic. We soon learn to be afraid of things that could hurt us. Such fear becomes the teacher that imparts common sense to our understanding.

But, as with every good gift of God, Satan will seek to distort the truth and hold us in bondage. So, when we have a frightening experience, we don't always just learn a good lesson from what we have gone through, Satan will seek to use that experience to lock our thinking and our emotions into the trauma of the event.

Fear, then, can become an easy entry point for demons when people go through a traumatic experience. Fear of the unknown, fear of what's going to happen next, fear of dying, fear of a hundred and one different things that can grip the heart of man from time to time can be used by Satan to control people. Fear controls vast areas of some people's lives, and spirits of fear thrive on the opportunities that fear can create.

When someone is controlled by irrational fear, there is almost always a demonic stronghold behind the manifesting behaviour. In the Scriptures, Jesus is described as perfect love, and the Scripture tells us that *"perfect love casts out fear"* (1 John 4:18). It is only in the name of Jesus that the power of the spirit of fear can be broken. And when the rights that gave the enemy the opportunity to come in have been undermined, it can be cast out.

The roots and causes of harmful fears

Irrational fears, such as those listed above, can often begin as a rational response to something we don't like. Most of us, for example, don't like wasps, but some people go phobic (manifest extreme fear and consequential behaviour) when they see a wasp fly into the room. Such people have usually had a traumatic experience with a wasp that stung them For them it is a totally rational response to be afraid of wasps. Or they could even have known someone who reacted so badly to the sting that it caused a major condition or, even, proved fatal. Such circumstances could well open a person up to receive a spirit which latched on to the fear.

One lady came for prayer because she had a fear of flying and she was about to go on a journey which necessitated a flight. In reality, it wasn't flying she was afraid of, it was crashing. Not long before, she had seen the devastating remains of a terrible air crash on television. She got so involved in watching the pictures on TV that fear of what would happen to her if the plane crashed gripped and controlled her.

On the 11th September 2001, I was standing at the check-in counter at Toronto airport, when all the computers were suddenly closed down and all flights were cancelled. It was the moment that two aeroplanes had been flown deliberately into the twin towers in New York. I walked across to the hotel lobby and stood with dozens of other shocked and traumatised travellers as we watched on TV the horrendous scene unfolding. Through watching those video clips time and time again many people succumbed to a spirit of fear – fear of being the victim of a terrorist attack, especially in the air.

Sometimes people have a fear of something, but they have no idea where it came from, making it difficult to deal with the problem, especially if there is a need to forgive someone. One lady knew that all the spiders she would encounter in the UK were totally harmless. But that didn't prevent her from being totally phobic at the sight of a spider anywhere near her. It wasn't until the Lord exposed the inner brokenness caused by trauma through deliberate childhood cruelty, in which her parents subjected her to spiders crawling all over herbody, that we knew why she was so terrified of them. The Lord both healed her brokenness and delivered her from the fear, so that spiders were no longer a threat to her.

On one occasion, a lady who had come for prayer reacted very badly to the ministry team who had been assigned to her on a Healing Retreat. The man in the team was very kind and loving, but he had a moustache and the thought of being prayed for by a man with a moustache was more than she could stand. She had a totally irrational fear of men with a moustache. The root of this fear was in her childhood when a man with a moustache had sexually abused her and her irrational subconscious conclusion was that all men with moustaches are abusers! The Lord used her reaction to help direct the team in how to pray with her.

These few examples illustrate how there can be hundreds of different root causes for fears that can be utterly controlling and debilitating. Satan is described in Scripture as a thief and a robber (John 10:10). And I have seen all too often how he has used fear to so dominate someone that they are robbed of being able to enjoy life to the full. They are in captivity – but the good news is that Jesus came to set the captives free!

Learning to live in a new way

One of the problems with fears is that they can become so much a part of our daily living that a fearful response has now become learned behaviour. It's as if the behaviour has become part of our identity when, in reality, it is not how God made us to be.

Deliverance may be an important part of the healing process, but deliverance has then got to be followed up by our choosing to walk out of the learned behaviour patterns and cease to be controlled in the way we have been in the past. It's as if, in the past, we have been living within the constrictions of a behaviour mould, and now that the constricting mould has been confessed and removed we are still allowing ourselves to be conformed to the limitations of its shape.

Romans 8:29 tells us that, as believers, we are *"predestined to be conformed to the image of his Son"*. And that means that, in Christ, we can break free from the learned behaviour of our past and allow our lives, personalities and character to become more and more shaped by the character of Jesus. The perfect freedom that Christ brings is the liberty that God gives us not to be controlled by the enemy's wishes, but to be freed to be our real selves and to go and do the things that Jesus has prepared for us (Ephesians 2:10). That is our destiny and there is no need to be afraid when Jesus takes us by the hand into His future for us.

There will be times when we face a situation that formerly we would have shied away from because of fear. So, when all the old reactions begin to surface, we need not think it's because God hasn't healed or delivered us, it's a bit like one of those memory foam mattresses which remembers the shape of your body! That 'spiritual memory foam' has remembered that you used to be afraid of whatever it is you are facing and so you react accordingly!

It's at that point you need to make a simple decision – to remember that the Holy Spirit is with you, choose not to be afraid and press on, trusting in the protection of Jesus. As you do so the Lord will reshape your 'memory foam' and the fear pattern will quickly give way to a new pattern of living God's way.

Fear free!

There may be other fears in your life which you will still need to deal with, but having seen and experienced how God has set you free from one fear, you will know that God will be able to set you free from whatever else is still affecting you in this way. It's not unusual for fearful people to have several fears, for vulnerability to one fear makes you sensitive to others. And little by little a succession of fears may have become like the bars of a cage holding you in bondage.

Now is the time for you to step out boldly on a faith journey of overcoming your own learned behaviour and being set free from any demonic control. The road to freedom is sometimes like a journey, where you take one step at a time into your future. With each new step of faith, the shackles of irrational fears slip away and little by little you become the person God intended you to be.

You are now in a place to respond unconditionally to the direction of the Lord in your life, knowing that no fears need stand in the way of God's purposes for your life. The third verse of that wonderful old hymn, *Just as I am*, by Charlotte Elliot, expresses her own vulnerability and tells how her coming to Jesus, just as she was, proved to be the God-given remedy.

Just as I am—though tossed about
With many a conflict, many a doubt,
Fightings and fears within, without—
O Lamb of God, I come, I come.

Charlotte Elliot describes the *"Fightings and fears, within without"* which in Christ she overcame as Jesus broke every barrier down. To be fear free is to be in Christ – and to be in Christ is to be fear free!

It is truly amazing to see the difference in people's lives when the fear that has been controlling them (often for most of their lives) has been cast out and they are free to be themselves. I have seen people healed so that they are suddenly able to drive again, fly in an aircraft, relate with people they were frightened of, eat food they had previously associated with some frightening experience, able to have sexual intercourse again with their husbands or wives and many, many more similar things. Christians have a tremendous responsibility to minister the healing love of Jesus into people's lives so that fear is no longer the false god that determines their life pattern and behaviour. It truly is through the perfect love of Jesus that fears are cast out and overcome (1 John 4:13).

A Prayer to Help You

I recognise, Lord, that You are holy. And I want to live my life in awe and reverence of the Creator of the Universe who loved me so much that He sent His Son to die for me. I want to have a holy fear of stepping outside Your will for my life and of not doing those things that You have prepared me for.

But I recognise, also, that there can be ungodly fears of things that I don't need to be afraid of. Fears that have their origin in some of the bad things that I have experienced or things that I have learned to be afraid of from others such as my Mum or my Dad.

I thank You, Lord, that Your Word tells me Your perfect love casts out all fear, that my life is in Your hands and that I do not need to be afraid. So, I want to bring to you now all those irrational things that I have learned to be afraid of. I name them before

You now and give them into Your hands. I now take authority over spirits of fear that Satan has been using to control my life. In the Name of Jesus I order them to leave me now.

Thank You Jesus that You are the only one who can truly set the captives free! Amen

CHAPTER 10

Learning to Live Again

Discovering God's purposes for your life

God has a purpose for the life of each one of us – and we don't need to do or achieve anything to be loved by Him! In that one sentence, we have the parameters of Kingdom living – a destiny to fulfil and being unconditionally loved! A destiny which gives us value and purpose (Jeremiah 29:11) and unconditional love in which we can blossom and flourish as we live and move and have our being (Acts 17:28). Or, as Isaiah 49:16 puts it, *"See, I have engraved you on the palms of my hands."* When God holds out His hands towards mankind, your name is there in His embrace and inside that embrace you are safe!

When a child grows through all the stages of being parented – from conception to maturity – knowing that they are loved, wanted, provided for and protected, they experience the freedom to make the very best of their future lives. And when we have come to the Lord ourselves at whatever stage of life we are at, and receive new life when we are born again, and then allow Him to heal us step by step, it's as if God puts 'the clay of our lives' back on the potter's wheel and reveals and restores our true destiny for us to walk in.

Jeremiah 18:6 expresses this so beautifully, applying this illustration to the nation of Israel, *"Can I not do with you, Israel, as this potter does?"* declares the LORD. *"Like clay in the hand of the potter, so are you in my hand, Israel."* If God can do that with a nation, so He can do it with you and your life – give you a fresh start as you step forward into the first day of the rest of your lives. For many people, it is like learning to live again, breathing the fresh new air of the Kingdom of God. That is the heart and purpose of this book.

Living as children of the Kingdom of God, our lives can become a powerful witness to the presence and power of God. A transformed life demonstrates a clear message of hope to our family, friends and neighbours – those we meet and live out our lives with every day.

When Paul was telling people about his life of ministry in Romans 15:18-19, he said that all he had accomplished was only through the signs and wonders and the mighty power of the Holy Spirit of God. People heard his message and they saw the outworking of God's presence and power.

Today God is restoring His people because He loves them, and each restored life becomes a lighthouse of truth shining into a desperately needy world. In today's multi-faith world, traditional evangelism may have lost some of its acceptability, but the message of hope and healing is a message which will speak to the devotees of any and every religion.

Every human being, whatever their beliefs or faith that they practice, has needs which only Jesus can meet. And when Jesus has met you at your point of need then you have a story to tell your family, your friends and your neighbours. And when they ask the questions about what has happened to you, then your answer will be listened to. This is one of the reasons why God has been raising up the healing ministry in our generation, because it is a salvation message unlike any other – a powerful evangelistic statement.

When the woman who Jesus met at the well in Samaria went back to her village, she had been so transformed by the encounter that *"Many of the Samaritans from that town believed in him because of the woman's testimony"* (John 4:39). And when they listened themselves to what Jesus had to say *"many more became believers . . . we know that this man really is the Saviour of the world"* (John 4:41 and 42).

Forgetting what's behind

The Apostle Paul was an amazing and very educated man. He became the lead missionary of the apostolic age, but he had a past! Before his conversion he was so filled with hatred of believing Christians that he became complicit in the murder of Stephen. But God met him on the road to Damascus and his whole life was turned around.

Even though Paul had had a personal encounter with Jesus, it would have been very easy for him to be so ashamed of his past that he could never do anything positive in his future. He could have fallen into the same trap as Simon Peter did at first – he went back to his fishing after betraying Jesus three times!

But Paul had come full circle – while he would never be able to deny the facts about his past and what he did, he was determined to forget what was behind him in another way and not let his past be an obstacle to his future calling. So, he said, *"I press on to take hold of that for which Christ Jesus took hold of me . . .*

forgetting what is behind and straining toward what is ahead" (from Philippians3:12-13).

There was a calling on Paul's life. But Paul was not unique – for there is a calling on each and every one of our lives. The Word of God encourages us to follow in Paul's footsteps and even though we cannot change the events of our personal history, nevertheless, once God has healed us of our past, we truly no longer need to let any of those things stand in the way of our personal destiny in Christ Jesus.

John Newton was a notorious slave trader, but Christ met him in the midst of his evil trade, transformed his life and he went on to have a profound ministry for the rest of his days. The words of his song, *Amazing Grace,* have impacted the world for generations and will continue to do so till Jesus comes again.

So, don't entertain any thought that God can't use you to bless Him, His Church and His people. An old Christian song that I sang as a child includes the words, *"There's a work for Jesus none but you can do."*

> *There's a work for Jesus, ready at your hand,*
> *'Tis a task the Master just for you has planned.*
> *Haste to do His bidding, yield Him service true;*
> *There's a work for Jesus none but you can do.*

> *Refrain:*
> *Work for Jesus, day by day,*
> *Serve Him ever, falter never; Christ obey.*
> *Yield Him service loyal, true,*
> *There's a work for Jesus none but you can do.*

I believe that for you, absolutely, so be encouraged!

Discovering God's purpose for my life

Many people never discover the joy of walking in God's plans and purposes for their life. For many, the simple reason is that their lack of wholeness and need of healing has become a barrier, which limits their vision. They become blinded by the god of this world to such an extent that they cannot see the path that God lays out ahead of them.

But having walked through this book together, I am praying that God has opened your eyes to see those things that are in need of healing in your life and that you are now beginning to walk in the freedom that Jesus offers.

If that is your experience then this is a good moment, therefore, to take a fresh look at your life and everything that is connected with your family, your church fellowship and your personal life and circumstances. Ask Him to show you His way forward in every area.

One of the primary ways that God speaks to us is through His Word, the Bible. I would strongly encourage you, if you are not already doing so, to start taking time each day to simply read Scripture and ask the Holy Spirit to speak to you through it. I have already shared how, as a child, my parents taught me to read from the Bible every day. I'm sure there was much I didn't understand, but because I got it into my mind when I was young, much of it is still there now, even though I am very much older. I am still drawing on the resources that were put into my spiritual bank account in those early days of my life! The Bible is food for the spirit and food for the soul and if we adhere to the scriptural principles of living, it will prove to be good for the body as well!

Psalm 119:105 says, *"Your word is a lamp to my feet and a light for my path."* As we read it we discover that the Bible is ***God's*** *revelation* to man of the truth about Himself. It is, therefore, the most precious book ever written.

It is a guide for living life to the full. It gives us a road map for the perilous journey of life. *It is a storehouse* of wonderful stories for children and grown-ups. *It is a refuge* in time of trouble. People in pain, in suffering, in prison, in mourning, tell how they turned to the Bible and found strength in their desperate hours. The truths of Scripture are a secure anchor on which we can trust.

The Bible is a sourcebook for everyday living. We find standards for our conduct, guidelines for knowing right from wrong, and principles to help us in a confused society where so often "anything goes."

In summary, the Bible is the most extraordinary book on the planet! It is the very Word of God to the human race. If we read it and apply its truths into our lives, it will be totally life-transforming. Every believer needs to take some time out every day to read something from its pages. The instruction to *"read, mark, learn and inwardly digest"* is never applied more appropriatelyt than to the Word of God.

And as we pray into all the things that God shows us from His Word, we will discover Him leading us one step at a time into His purposes for the next season of our lives. *Discovering Healing and Freedom* is not just about healing – it is also about preparing our heart for the days ahead.

Pressing on towards the goal

Having chosen not to be limited by his past, Paul was determined to press on *"towards the goal to win the prize for which God has called me heavenward in Christ Jesus"* (Philippians 3:14). Paul had learned to have his focus firmly fixed on two objectives – firstly the fulfilment of his destiny here on earth – but ahead of that was the heavenly reward which awaited him in glory.

As believers, we are blessed by being able to walk with the Lord day by day while here on earth – but we have lying ahead of us a prize, which Paul describes as his upward calling to Heaven's glory. And what a prize and reward that is to look forward to.

The disciples were concerned about the fact that Jesus was going to leave them, but Jesus' reply to their concerns has brought comfort to every generation of believers for the past two thousand years. He said, *"I am going to prepare a place for you, and take you to be with me"* (John 14:2-3). We have a home to go to – and, as Paul reminded us, *"No eye has seen, no ear has heard, no mind has conceived what God has prepared for those who love him"* (1 Corinthians 2:9).

Realising my destiny

God has always led His people forward by giving them vision for their future. I would encourage you, therefore, to keep a personal diary or journal of your walk with the Lord from this point on. Write down in your journal those things that you sense the Lord is showing you from His Word, or from your times of prayer. And when you believe the Lord has shown you the next step for your life share it and test it with someone you know and can really trust. They can then pray with you as you wait for the Lord to confirm what He is saying to you.

I will never forget the moment when God spoke into my life through a vision for the work that became known as Ellel Ministries. It was the second most important moment of my life. The most important was when I first gave my life to the Lord at the age of nine. But in this second key moment, God showed me in outline the work that He wanted me to do.

Sixteen years of daily praying were to follow before the work started, but every one of those years was part of God's precious preparation, even though, at times, I got very frustrated that nothing was happening sooner! But God's clocks kept perfect time for me, and so they will for you.

Just as the Lord eventually showed me the way ahead, as described in my book *Strands of Destiny*, the same God will guide and direct your steps as you allow Him to restore His order in your life. May the Lord go with you every step of the way as you press on to discover and fulfil the purposes which God has for you.

A Prayer to Help You

Thank You, Lord, that You have a plan and a purpose for my life. I no longer wish to let the previous events in my life be in control of my future. Thank You for all the healing You have already brought to me on this journey of discovery.

I recognise that there may be more healing that You want to bring to me. I am willing to let You have Your way in all the days that are left to me. I want each and every one to really count for You and Your Kingdom.

Help me, Lord, when I face challenges and temptations to look to You first for my comfort and encouragement, so that I will remain strong against all the attacks that Satan may bring against me. And when I do make mistakes help me to remember the wonderful promises from Your Word that if we do sin, then You are faithful and just and, because You paid the price for my sin, You will forgive and cleanse me when I come back to You in confession and repentance.

I pray that You will speak clearly to me in the days that lie ahead as I read Your Word and look to You for guidance in all the future decisions of my life. Help me to rediscover all the gifts and abilities that You gave me and which You want me to use.

I am so grateful for all You have done for me – may my life be a living witness to others of Your amazing love and mercy. In Jesus' Name, Amen.

Epilogue

When God first gave me a vision for healing, back in 1970, I had no concept of everything that He would include in the healing ministry. I didn't understand that the words for salvation and healing are the same and that, in God's eyes, healing was not just an add-on extra for when you're not feeling so good, but an absolutely fundamental constituent of what it means to be a disciple and follower of Jesus.

The fact is that because of the carnal nature of fallen humanity, we have all suffered the consequences of living in a sinful world and we are all, therefore, in need of healing! Through *Discover Healing and Freedom* we have been able to look at some of the issues that create problems for which we need God's healing and, sometimes, His deliverance.

The gift of salvation means that from the moment we enter into the Kingdom of God we begin to enjoy eternal life, so that death, when it comes, is simply a transition from life on Earth to life in Heaven. But the gift of healing is part of what Jesus meant when He asked disciples to pray *'Your Kingdom come – on Earth'*. For the ministry of healing is needed here on Earth – we definitely won't need it in Heaven! Healing brings the reality of God's love, power and presence into the experience of believers today.

Having completed this book you may like to think about learning more about healing – especially if there are still unresolved issues in your life or you would like to learn how to help others. For this reason, Ellel Ministries runs many different courses and training schools – especially the *Explore* series of courses. Information about *Explore* is given in the *Afterword,* but you can find out much more about this and everything else from Ellel Ministries by going to our website at www.ellel.org.

May the Lord richly bless and encourage you as you seek to live for Him day by day.

Afterword –
Time to Explore

If you have enjoyed reading this book, you may be wondering if there is another step you can take on your own personal journey of discovery and healing, so that you can learn more about all the topics covered. To meet this need Ellel Ministries International has established a regular programme of courses at all our centres, under the name *Explore.*

The ten courses of the Explore A programme include:

The Big Picture   Exploring God's Foundation
for Life

Knowing God   Exploring the Character and
Nature of God

God's Master Key   Exploring the Power of
Forgiveness

Lost and Found	Exploring the Remedy for Rejection
God's Enemy Exposed	Exploring Healing Through Deliverance
Inside Out Healing	Exploring Inner Damage and
Knowing Me	Exploring Restoration of the Human Spirit
Connected	Exploring God's Design for Relationships
Sheltered	Exploring the Antidote to Fear and Anxiety
Healing Workshop	Exploring Ministry Practice

Please visit our website (www.ellel.org) for details and dates of the *Explore Courses* which are available at an Ellel Centre near you. There is also a second series of **Explore Courses** (Explore B) for those who have completed *Explore A*.

In addition to **Explore**, there are many other short courses designed to help those with different personal issues and to train people in how to bring God's healing to others. Full details of all these courses are to be found on our website at www.ellel.org

You may also like to consider attending a longer-term training school at one of our Centres in the UK. These include the **20-day Impact School** at Ellel Scotland, the **9-week Flagship School** at Ellel Grange and the longer **NETS Training Programme** at Ellel Pierrepont.

About The Author

Peter Horrobin is the Founder and International Director of Ellel Ministries International, which began in 1986 as a ministry of healing in the north-west of England. The work is now established in over thirty-five different countries, providing teaching, training and personal ministry opportunities. (www.ellel.org)

After graduating from Oxford University with a degree in Chemistry, Peter spent a number of years lecturing in College and University, before leaving the academic environment for the world of business. Here he founded a series of successful publishing and bookselling companies.

In his twenties he started to restore a vintage sports car (an Alvis Speed 20) but discovered that its chassis was bent. As he looked at the broken vehicle, wondering if it could ever be repaired, he sensed God asking him a question, "You could restore this broken car, but I can restore broken lives. Which is more important?" It was obvious that broken lives were more important than broken cars and so the beginnings of a vision for healing and restoration was birthed in his heart.

A hallmark of Peter's ministry has been his willingness to step out in faith and see God move to fulfil His promises, often in remarkable ways. His book, Strands of Destiny, tells many of the amazing stories of what God has done in the past thirty years.

Peter has written many books including The Complete Catalogue of British Cars. And for the past thirty-five years he has been the editor of Mission Praise, one of the largest-selling hymn and song books in the UK and originally compiled for the visit of Billy Graham in 1984.

In this season of their lives, Peter, and his wife Fiona are concentrating on writing so that all their knowledge and experience can be made permanently available in book form through Sovereign World Ltd and other publishers around the world. His book Healing Through Deliverance is now a Christian classic.

Further books by Peter Horrobin

Journey to Freedom Book Series

In this remarkable series of books, Peter takes the reader on a step-by-step journey of personal transformation – one day at a time. Originally produce as on-line daily teaching, Peter has now re-edited the whole material into a very accessible book format. The restoration of God's order in a person's life is Peter's objective as this is the foundation for both healing and discipleship.

8-part book series. 256 – 368 pages per book. £16.99 each

Strands of Destiny

Peter Horrobin's personal account of how God envisioned him through the remains of a crashed car, to establish the healing work of Ellel Ministries at Ellel Grange, will build your faith as you journey with him through the ups and downs of what became a world-wide spiritual adventure.

Paperback 464 pages plus 48 pages of colour photographs, £14.99,

ISBN 978-1-85240-835-0

Forgiveness – God's Master Key

Forgiveness is key to the restoration of our relationship with God and to healing from the consequences of hurtful, damaging human relationships. This book is one of the most outstanding and concise available on the subject of forgiveness.

Paperback 110 pages, £6.99, ISBN 978-1-85240-502-1

Living Life God's Way

Living Life God's Way is an immensely readable and practical book. In this revised and updated edition of *Living the Life – Practical Christianity for the Real World*, Peter Horrobin guides you through a landscape of hidden truths. Using real life testimonies, parables and illustrations to unlock some of the most difficult of life's issues that often make us stumble through our Christian walk. This book was written to help new Christians get established in their faith and to provide older Christians with the kind of realistic help that is needed to keep their lives on track with God.

Paperback 222 pages, £10.99, ISBN 978-1-85240-758-2

Healing Through Deliverance

The Foundation and Practice of Deliverance Ministry

In this comprehensive, practical and ground-breaking volume, Peter draws on this extensive experience to set out a thorough and scriptural foundation for the healing and deliverance ministry – an integral part of fulfilling the Great Commission and a vital key to discipleship. This authoritative handbook will equip you to understand and respond to the call of God to set the captives free. A classic.

Hardback 630 pages, £24.99, ISBN 978-1-85240-498-7

Healing from the Consequences of Accident, Shock and Trauma

Unhealed trauma is one of the primary reasons why some people do not easily heal from the consequences of accidents or sudden shocks. This ground-breaking book is the culmination of thirty years of experience praying for such people. This foundational teaching has been instrumental in bringing permanent healing to people all over the world.

Paperback 176 pages, £9.99, ISBN 978-1-85240-743-8

The Truth and freedom Series

All the books in this series have been written by members of the Ellel Ministries Teams. Each one highlights a particular topic that has proved to be of significance in the lives of those who have come on our Healing Retreats. When we get God's truth into our hearts, He ministers His freedom into our lives.

Anger, How do you handle it?

Paperback, 112 pages, Paul and Liz Griffin, ISBN 978-1-85240-450-7

God's Covering, A Place of Healing

Paperback, 192 pages, David Cross, ISBN 978-1-85240-485-7

God's Way out of Depression

Paperback, 160 pages, David Cross ISBN 978-1-85240-809-1

Hope and Healing for the Abused

Paperback, 128 pages, Paul and Liz Griffin, ISBN 978-1-85240-480-2

Intercession & Healing, Breaking Through with God

Paperback, 176 pages, Fiona Horrobin, ISBN 978-1-85240-500-7

Rescue from Rejection, Finding Security in God's Loving Acceptance

Paperback, 160 pages, Denise Cross, ISBN 978-1-85240-555-7

Soul Ties, The Unseen Bond in Relationships

Paperback, 128 pages, David Cross, ISBN 978-1-85240-597-7

Stepping Stones to the Father Heart of God

Paperback, 176 pages, Margaret Silvester, ISBN 978-1-85240-623-3

The Dangers of Alternative Ways of Healing, How to Avoid New Age Deceptions

Paperback, 176 pages, David Cross & John Berry, ISBN 978-1-85240-537-3

Trapped by Control, How to Find Freedom

Paperback, 112 pages, David Cross, ISBN 978-1-85240-501-4

For more details about all these books
and ordering information
please go to:
www.sovereignworld.com
or visit the store at
www.ellel.org

ABOUT ELLEL MINISTRIES
www.ellel.org
OUR VISION

Ellel Ministries is a non-denominational Christian Mission Organization with a vision to resource and equip the Church by welcoming people, teaching them about the Kingdom of God and healing those in need (Luke 9:11).

OUR MISSION
Our mission is to fulfil the above vision throughout the world, as God opens the doors, in accordance with the Great Commission of Jesus and the calling of the Church to proclaim the Kingdom of God by preaching the good news, healing the broken-hearted and setting the captives free. We are, therefore, committed to evangelism, healing, deliverance, discipleship and training. The particular scriptures on which our mission is founded are **Isaiah 61:1–7; Matthew 28:18–20; Luke 9:1–2, 9:11; Ephesians 4:12; 2 Timothy 2:2.**

OUR BASIS OF FAITH
God is a Trinity. God the Father loves all people. God the Son, Jesus Christ, is Saviour and Healer, Lord and King. God the Holy Spirit indwells Christians and imparts the dynamic power by which they are enabled to continue Christ's ministry. The Bible is the divinely inspired authority in matters of faith, doctrine and conduct, and is the basis for teaching.

Ellel Ministries International
Ellel Grange
Ellel
Lancaster, LA2 0HN
United Kingdom